RISE.

THE 4-WAY MANIFESTO FOR LIFE & LEGACY

BECOME YOUR NEXT BEST SELF
RISE. The 4-Way Manifesto for Life & Legacy

Copyright © 2020 Patricia Murugami

ISBN 978 - 9966 - 69 - 049 - 4

Published by

PUBLISHING
Institute of Africa

P.O. Box 16458 - 00100

NAIROBI, KENYA

info@publishing-institute.org

www.publishing-institute.org

Some of the stories and incidents depicted in this book are true, and others are a work of fiction. Any resemblance to actual persons, living or dead, events, business entities or localities is entirely coincidental or used fictitiously without any intent to describe their actual conduct.

Printed in Kenya.

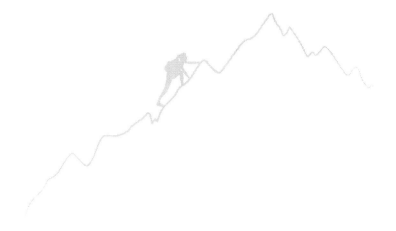

Dedication

To my husband, Murugami, you are my pillar, sounding board, friend, and covenant love.

To each of our children, you are special gifts; your creativity, youthful spirit, and talents inspire me.

To my parents, Cecilia and Ephraim Kariithi, you sacrificed to educate me and have been a beacon of light both personally and professionally.

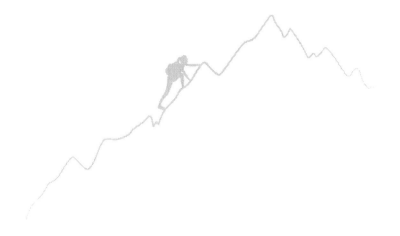

Acknowledgements

To my family—my husband, children, parents and siblings;

To my team at Breakthrough Leadership Transformation;

To my friends and clients;

To the publishing team led by Dr Kirimi Barine, Esther, and the entire team;

Asanteni sana!

This would not have been possible without each of you.

Table of Contents

Preface

What is my purpose? How do I find my divine assignment? What can I do to get more out of my life? How can I become the best version of me? If I had a dollar for every time someone has asked me these questions, I'd have retired to some idyllic beach resort in a beautiful part of my country, Kenya.

After many years of struggling to find my unique calling and trying to align my professional work to that inner quest, I have found that there are ways in which you can start to climb the proverbial mountain and swim through the deepest seas (you can see I am an avid fan of **The Sound of Music** and Maria's epic performance of 'Climb Every Mountain') to become **your next best self.**

'Your' refers to you, as only **you** can intentionally choose to change yourself.

'Next' refers to the natural progression to grow; metamorphosis; the state of change.

'Best' refers to the higher, purer, more sublime state of growth. Our best continues to evolve as we conquer our weaknesses and understand ourselves (and others) better. In other words, my best last year is not my best this year.

'Self' refers to your inner and outer being, that is, your body, mind, heart, and soul.

To help you reflect as you seek to grow and become your next best self, I **developed** a four-dimensional leadership model summarised as **G=H⁴** where:

G refers to growth. It is the kind of growth that permeates every aspect of your life, that is, growth of your body, mind, heart, and soul. This growth is both personal and professional. It is inside out—focusing on the internal aspects before the external aspects.

H⁴ refers to the ability to raise different dimensions of your leadership in a transformative way. These four aspects—heart, head, hand, and higher purpose, when raised, will lead to intentional impact, transformation, service, and becoming your next best self.

The G=H⁴ model is a guide to help you become your next best self and raise your BAR (behaviour change based on a paradigm shift in your **b**eliefs, attitudes, and consequently results).

My prayer is that as you read this book, you will find clarity of purpose, courage to carry out your purposeful vision, and conviction to change your behaviours and attitudes to achieve your goals and become your next best self.

A short while ago, a senior leader who was a colleague earlier on in my career said to me, 'Patricia, what incredible growth you have achieved: from an accountant to a leadership guru!' As I thanked him and said I was not a guru yet, it dawned on me my journey has been one of fear and faith, courage and weakness, starting and ending, clarity and confusion, and painful reinvention. Through the struggles, doubt, shame, guilt, joy, faith, hope, and peace, my journey of growth continues. I invite you to take time to reflect on your life experiences, glean the lessons, choose to be better and not bitter, and start your journey of growth to become your next best self.

THE
FIRST LEVEL

The Power of Raising Your Heart

The first H in our G=H⁴ model refers to raising the heart. The wisdom of Proverbs 4:23 says that all things emanate from the heart. Thus, examining your heart— *what weighs it down and what lifts it up*—lays the foundation for the journey.

Raising the heart entails intentional growth of character and habits of excellence, which some researchers call the character quotient. It includes the ability to grow your self-awareness, and know, regulate, and master virtues like courage, hope, authenticity, humility, generosity, and patience. Raising your heart also incorporates nurturing your emotional, relational, and social intelligence.

Most of the decisions we make come from our heart influenced by our head. This means your ability to know yourself, guard your heart, and stretch yourself to grow, based on your vision and dreams, all start from your heart.

Whose Shoulders Are You Standing On?

If I have seen further than others, it is by standing upon the shoulders of giants.

~ **Isaac Newton**

When I think of my own life and leadership experiences, it all began at home with the example and presence of my mum and dad. Our parents instilled a deep sense of belonging in our family and intentionally taught us the values of hard work, excellence, and follow-through based on Christian virtues.

Recently, I turned on the television and found the rainbow-coloured stripes and sharp shrill sound that instantly reminded me of my teenage years when the only television station available to us (the Voice of Kenya, VOK) began broadcasting at 4pm and closed at 10pm *(if you were born after the year 2000, you are probably wondering what planet I came from, but that was the life we had)*. To earn the privilege of watching a TV show, we had to complete our chores punctually and with excellence. These included but were not limited to home cleaning, taking care of the pigs, chicken, rabbits, weeding, planting, harvesting, and my all-time non-favourite—cooking for the dogs and collecting their daily entrails.

The holidays for my siblings and I sometimes felt like drudgery. As teenagers, our chores looked like corporal punishment as all our peers were having fun while our parents fully occupied us with household chores and farm work. Some of them went as far as teasing and calling us derogatory names. It was painful and we felt that we did not belong in the in-crowd. We felt like outcasts in our young peer society and thought our parents were unfair and unreasonable. My mummy would say in response to our moody call for justice that hard work never killed anyone and proceed to mesh out additional chores when we complained to prove her point. Together with my two younger brothers, we would opt to stop complaining and work better and faster.

Looking back with the benefit of hindsight, I see the value of the pain and lessons, and I realise that my parents' shoulders, which I mistakenly thought were painful shoulders, are the giant shoulders upon which I stood on, and continue to stand on, to see further and have more impact. Our home was my first school of life and leadership, and I am forever grateful for the daily lessons our parents taught us not only by words but also by deeds to date.

Fast-forward 20 years later, when I began working, I met demanding bosses who raised my standard of work ethic by insisting on excellence through fear-based management. I had managers who threw physical files and documents back at me in front of other colleagues to ensure we worked better and finished well. At the time, I struggled to find the lesson behind that pain as I fought back tears of humiliation. There are teachers, mentors, bosses, clients, coaches, and friends who have been the shoulders upon which I stand. The experiences were not always rosy, and at the time, it was not always clear I was being prepared for my future growth, but I now see that each experience was to teach me a life lesson.

Unfortunately, I was not always a student ready to learn, but the following lessons continue to serve me well:

» The importance of keeping your word.

» The habit of delaying gratification.

» Finishing things well even when the initial excitement has waned.

» The power of not giving in to peer pressure and focusing on what matters, like maintaining positive and strong family bonds.

» Cultivating a culture of excellence, regardless of the significance or size of the task.

My experiences continue to birth new lessons now that I am a parent. Together with my husband Murugami, we continue to pass on these lessons to our children and future generations.

Many life lessons come wrapped like gifts while other times, the packaging is not as attractive. Unless we cultivate the habit of reflecting and discerning the lesson behind the wrapping, with an attitude of gratitude for all we go through—the good, the bad, the

ugly, the painful, the messy, the shameful, and the wonderful—
we are not likely to learn from our experiences and cannot grow.

I don't believe that experience is your best teacher; experience
reflected upon is your best teacher. Becoming your next best self
begins with using a lens of reflection and appreciation for all you
have been through and the milestones you have achieved thus
far. Authentic learners inculcate the spirit of gratitude because
they view the experiences they have undergone to be part of
the practical school of life and as a result, they become their next
best selves.

How grateful are you for who you are today?

According to a Harvard Health article titled, 'Giving thanks can
make you happier', a person with a grateful heart is likely to be
more open to growth and receive more opportunities than the
ungrateful one. The difference between the two is not what life
throws at them, but how they take life and glean lessons with a
thankful spirit.

BREAKTHROUGH COACHING

1. Take some time to quietly look back at your life. Make a list of individuals who have helped you grow through painful and positive experiences (social, career, spiritual, etc.).

   Painful shoulders:

   - Paros
   - s/ teachers

   Positive shoulders:

   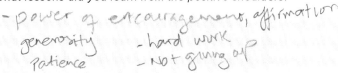

   - Mr mugambi   mama ndungu   Princess
   - mrs omoto   Tate ngoyo
   - mrs Gikonyo   mama Jane
   - mrs muhoro   Chapel - mary, bea

2. What lessons did you learn from the painful shoulders?

   - hard work   - farming
   - resilience   - child love
   - trust   - life skills
   - obedience   - generosity

3. What lessons did you learn from the positive shoulders?

   - power of encouragement, affirmation
     generosity   - hard work
       patience   - Not giving up

4. Write your gratitude list below:

   - life   home   - friends
   - health   family   - word
   - boys   security   - apps
   - peace   community   - tech

5. Commit to contact at least two names on your list with a word or token of appreciation for their contribution in making you the person you are today.

Know Thyself

Knowing yourself is the beginning of all wisdom.

~ **Aristotle**

When I conduct leadership programmes and ask my clients to do a personal SWOT (strengths, weaknesses, opportunities, and threats) analysis, the typical reaction is some level of discomfort as people normally associate SWOT analysis with work-related projects. As you journey to become your next best self, it is important to carry out a personal SWOT analysis.

Samuel Otuke, a senior leader in one of my leadership programs, took the SWOT exercise seriously and asked his children to give him feedback. He was pleasantly affirmed when they told him how they liked it when he played with them— albeit rarely. When the children mentioned his iPad and phones as his weakness, saying they wished they were his mobile phone because he held it and gave it so much attention, Samuel was shocked. He committed to change his ways radically by leaving the gadgets in his car when he got home.

Samuel is not alone. As I was building Breakthrough Leadership Transformation in the initial years, I spent so much time on my phone that it was taking over my family and personal time. I was at the point of near nomophobia or smartphone addiction. My family was complaining. My personal rituals of meditation and exercise were getting the dregs of the day. And worse still, I knew I could not teach and coach one thing in my self-knowledge and mastery class and live out a different thing. I remembered Samuel's commitment and decided to do the very same thing. When I got home, I would leave my phone in the car. Out of sight is out of mind right? It worked.

The first day I was itching like someone with an allergy to go to my car and get it. Once I overcame the temptation, I forgot and immersed myself in the activities I so valued but had neglected. I learnt how to single-task rather than multi-task. I felt like a tremendous weight had been lifted off my shoulders— the weight of the expectation to respond or deal with each message almost instantly, and the discomfort this brought to my family and personal time. This change came from a simple, yet intense, exercise to get to know myself.

Take a moment to reflect deeply on all you are and all that you have become, from the very random and minuscule, to the more profound.

DO YOU KNOW WHO YOU ARE? NOT WHAT YOU DO. WHO YOU ARE?

The first time I reflected upon that question, I felt lost. Many of my clients and networks struggle with this question too. Yet it is the foundation of all growth.

Who are you stripped of your titles and roles? Who are you without your profession, achievements, and accolades?

Let's start the journey of getting to know you.

If you are like me, and I know I am in good company, many times, people complain that others do not understand them. Today, I want you to shift your focus, clear your lens and turn the question to yourself. Do you understand yourself?

To answer this question, you need to start by conducting a personal SWOT analysis. We begin by getting to know our current strengths and areas of growth.

IDENTIFY YOUR STRENGTHS

In their Strengthsfinder 2.0 book, Gallup's definition of a strength is 'a consistent near perfect performance in an activity'.

How do you identify your strengths?

- » Think about genuine compliments you have received from others.
- » Think about times when you have done work that was so enjoyable you were in a state of flow.
- » Think about times when you have done what others consider difficult but for you it feels effortless.
- » Think about times when you have done something that fills you internally with joy and peace and a sense of deep fulfilment.

[handwritten margin notes: Intentional, resilience, Photo, Cook, encouragement, insight, adaptive, Determined, organised, P+ skills]

» What are those experiences, and what strengths emerge as you consider your responses?

» Can you list at least ten strengths that you have?

KNOW YOUR WEAKNESSES

A weakness is a habit or action that prevents you from growing and improving. A weakness can also emanate from excessive use of a strength. In positive psychology, it is known as an opportunity for growth.

How do you get to know your weaknesses?

[handwritten margin notes: - fear, - unforgiveness, - underestimate, capabilities, - language (public speaking)]

» Consider those habits holding you back from doing the things you know you ought to do.

» Think about comments and critique you have received from others on areas you can develop.

» What are the 5 weaknesses that prevent you from becoming your next best self?

LOOK OUT FOR OPPORTUNITIES

[handwritten margin notes: - career break, - Training, - UX, - Internet, - networks, - contacts, - webinars, - Books]

Opportunities are possibilities external to us that present a chance for potential growth and expansion. They include a learning chance, a project you can undertake, a new role or responsibility, or any other positive possibility you can undertake to move forward.

Write five opportunities in the short-, medium-, and long-term horizon available for you to consider, as you become your next best self.

CONSIDER YOUR THREATS

[handwritten margin notes: Procrastination, fear, Pandemic, poor health, others around me, Business]

Threats are challenging circumstances that are external to us that could prevent us from growing and leading ourselves better. Threats could include global pandemics such as COVID-19, wars, climate change, retrenchments, re-organisations, industry changes or even betrayals.

What are five threats that could potentially prevent you from becoming your next best self?

After conducting your personal reflection on your SWOT analysis, I invite you to ask several people in your personal and professional circles to give you candid feedback on what they see as your strengths, weaknesses, opportunities, and threats.

As they give you this feedback, it may be surprising, affirming, shocking or disappointing. I encourage you to see the feedback as a gift. Do not be defensive; ask for clarity and thank them sincerely for their feedback.

Once you have considered your personal SWOT, reflect on the following questions:

» Are you a friend to yourself?

» What can you do to appreciate yourself?

» Do you like spending time on your own? (That is the first measure of befriending yourself.)

BREAKTHROUGH COACHING

1. *Take time to do your personal SWOT analysis.*

INTERNAL FOCUS	EXTERNAL FOCUS
From within me	*From beyond me*
STRENGTHS	OPPORTUNITIES
WEAKNESSES	THREATS

2. *What did you learn from your personal SWOT that can help you move forward to become your next best self?*

3. *What do you commit to do after completing your SWOT?*

Who Is Sabotaging Your Efforts to Becoming Your Next Best Self?

Make sure your worst enemy is not living between your own two ears.

~ **Laird Hamilton.**

'They are out to get me! They have set me up to fail! They are the reason for my downfall! I have been victimised. Life is so unfair!'

These are the statements I have heard people make when life is not going as planned. My friend Mia Mala worked hard, and as she climbed the corporate ladder, she pursued opportunities to serve on a certain board. Finally, she received her appointment letter, and excitedly went to her first induction board meeting. As she confidently, yet apprehensively, walked into the boardroom, the older seasoned male board members with a smirk on their faces said, 'Oh, we now have a flower girl joining our board of directors.' They then went ahead to ask her during the first break to serve them tea and refreshments, to which she reluctantly served begrudgingly. Mia spent her first year on that board fighting within herself and despising her male colleagues for being unfair to her. She spent so much energy on survival mode, fighting for her rights, and trying to be perfect, that with hindsight, she did not gain as much experience as she would have had she had a different perspective.

Many years' later, Mia looks back at how she sabotaged herself and realises she could have sought a seasoned mentor, understood the board dynamics and with some humour and wisdom repositioned her role in the board. She could have attended a board leadership program and understood that behaviours such as mansplaining have a remedy. Mia recalls how she once shared her idea in a meeting, and the men in attendance did not 'hear' or acknowledge her contribution, in fact they ignored her. A few minutes later Mark, a fellow male board member shared the same idea under the guise that he was trying to explain what Mia had just said in a better way, and the other male board members received it with enthusiasm and commendations to Mark. Most women get angry and retreat sullenly into their corner as victims of mansplaining. What is mansplaining?

Mansplaining is defined as explaining something to someone in a way that suggests that they are stupid; used especially when a man explains something to a woman that she already understands.

I advised Mia to consider this remedy to mansplaining.

Instead of getting angry, with the knowledge that this happens and that she can do something about it, Mia should say:

'Mark thank you for echoing the idea I shared earlier. I welcome the idea of us working with the other board members to make it a reality to move the strategy forward.'

By reiterating you talked about the point or idea first, you take back your power. You do not do this to diminish the other person's power, but to help them realise what they are subconsciously doing—not acknowledging the ideas of the minorities.

From my own experience and doctoral research, there are many factors that hold us back from becoming our next best selves. However, the most sabotaging factors are not external barriers, they are the inner, internal barriers that hold us back from within. These limiting beliefs and habits keep many of us from knowing ourselves.

From my assessment, the top ten internal barriers to be aware of are:

1. Perfectionism
2. Procrastination
3. Messiah complex—super(wo)man syndrome
4. Ruminating on the past
5. Multitasking
6. Critical spirit
7. Imposter syndrome
8. Won't ask syndrome
9. Can't toot my horn syndrome (false modesty)
10. Toxic comparison

Let's look at each of these beliefs and habits in more detail.

Perfectionism

You may not know it, but perfectionism is the highest form of self-abuse. Yet, many times we talk about being a perfectionist as if we should be awarded a badge of honour for being one. Unfortunately, this habit has held back many people from becoming their next best selves.

Stephen Guise in his book, *How to Become an Imperfectionist* states that:

> *Perfectionists desire to act, look, and/or feel perfect. On a superficial level, it seems like something to be proud of, but not when you dig into the true implications of it. When you add 'ism' to the end of 'perfection' and 'imperfection', the natural connotations of the root words are reversed. Far from perfect, perfectionism is irrational, crippling, restrictive, and even lethal (e.g., anorexia and depression/suicide). If we fully grasped the reality of perfectionism's destructive influence on humanity, we would not be so eager and happy to label ourselves as perfectionists.*

Being a perfectionist will prevent you from becoming your next best self. Perfectionism means aiming for a high standard based on only your perspective and not considering the perspectives of others. Perfectionists never consider the journey but focus only on the destination. They never see what worked positively but instead focus on what did not work in any process until it cripples their progress. We should aim for excellence, not perfectionism.

Procrastination

This is the habit of putting off or delaying tasks that require immediate attention. Bishop Rosie O'neal states that procrastination is the arrogant assumption that God owes you another chance to do tomorrow what He gave you the chance to do today.

Brad Taylor says that procrastination is the grave in which

opportunity is buried.

Over the years, I have found that there are several types of procrastinators:

i. **The Scared Shawn**—he is afraid of taking responsibilities and avoids the responsibilities by pretending that he does not have the necessary skills.

ii. **The Angry Angela**—she keeps getting annoyed with her own self-induced delays and gets things done in the final moment with a high level of pressure.

iii. **The Crying Caren**—she does not like the idea of doing the task and resorts to emotional responses like crying to get out of the responsibility to complete the task assigned. Sometimes, this person is fearful of the task ahead and is unable to state that.

iv. **The FILO Fiona**—she takes tasks that were assigned last and prioritises them instead of prioritising the earlier tasks. Hence, applying the First In Last Out (FILO) method erroneously.

v. **The Hungry Henry**—when assigned a task, he resorts to comfort eating to avoid the notion of doing the task.

vi. **The Techie Tina**—she gets distracted with technology and social media, and avoids focusing on the task at hand.

vii. **The Perfect Peter**—he avoids doing the task unless the conditions to begin the task are perfect.

viii. **The High Pressure Purity**-—she takes pride in saying she does her best work under pressure and leaves tasks until the very last minute.

The antidote to all these types of procrastinators is to face their fear and begin the task immediately it is assigned.

Which kind of procrastinator are you?

Which task do you need to begin and finish well?

Messiah complex

When one has a Messiah complex, they believe they are responsible for saving or assisting others at any cost to themselves. From my coaching experience, I have found many people struggle with this complex, especially firstborn children who have a high sense of responsibility mixed with an unhealthy dose of perfectionism. A Messiah complex is the disabling ability to want to solve the problems of everyone around you and help them move forward without letting them take responsibility for their actions and progress. The Messiah complex also plagues high achievers who find it difficult to allow their team members to learn at their pace preferring to do their team's work as they believe they know how to do it better, and by doing their work, it will help them save time and effort in a bid to meet the deadline.

Ruminating on the past

Have you ever seen how cows ruminate as part of their digestion process? The human process of recalling negative past experiences, and mentally chewing on them is called rumination. Marshall Goldsmith and Sally Helgesen, authors of *How Women Rise,* state that this habit has a gender skew towards women more than men. They write:

> *Women not only spend more time reliving their setbacks, they are more likely to believe that whatever went wrong was their entire fault. It's a habit that does not serve women well.*

> *What you're actually doing is berating yourself, engaging in a kind of negative self-talk that can border on abuse.*

I suffered from this rumination habit for a long time and now see its link to perfectionism.

If something did not work out, as I wanted, I would rehash the issues over and over, trying to see how it should have gone according to my plan.

As I began my process of becoming a certified coach, the first person one learns to coach is oneself. I started to exercise more kindness towards myself and intentionally accept the outcomes. I continue to learn from younger children and reverse mentors to be more open and accepting of the outcomes.

» What might you be currently ruminating about?

» How does it make you feel every time you recall that failure?

» How can you shift that habit?

Multitasking

Multitasking is the ability to shift attention between two or more activities demanding your attention.

How many of us take great pride in being multitaskers?

Did you know that the more we multitask on matters that demand more attention, the more we cannot give any the right kind of attention?

I was a proud multitasker until I learnt that doing two things at once makes it impossible to be present for either because my attention was always fragmented, which then would minimise my output, impact, and presence.

In this hyper-connected era with the exponential use of digital tools, we have all being affected adversely with the reduced inability to concentrate.

According to the Journal of General Medicine, a research by Dr Naykky Ospina, found that patients had 11 seconds to explain the reasons for their visit before doctors interrupted or began multitasking while listening to them. The trend in hyper-distraction may be the reason why digital applications (apps) such as the fast-growing Tiktok app, only enable/allow videos of 15 seconds or less to get your undivided attention.

Women usually can multitask very well because of how our brains and emotions work, but sometimes it gets the worst of us.

» How many times over the last week have you been asked if you are paying attention?

» How many times have you made an error because you are trying to do two things at the same time?

» What would it take for you to single-task?

Multitasking is a negative habit that diminishes your impact and presence. It affects your ability to finish things well. Each of us can unlearn this saboteur by focusing on single tasking.

Critical spirit and negative self-talk

This critical internal spirit has a dramatic effect on how we see ourselves, speak to ourselves, and ultimately how we see others and react and respond to them.

A critical spirit is usually linked to perfectionism as we try to reach a self-imposed standard that we cannot reach effectively. As a result, we begin to put ourselves down by how we speak to ourselves. Did you know you are your most permanent and alert audience?

You are the one who hears everything you say to yourself and others. Dr Brene Brown in *Daring Greatly* poses this question, 'Would you speak to your best or closest friend the way you speak to yourself?'

This is a powerful way of learning positive self-talk.

Imposter syndrome

This syndrome makes us doubt ourselves, and our ability to do something meaningful. It normally appears before a significant decision. The only way to deal with imposter syndrome is to acknowledge you feel like a fraud but to not let it get the better of you or derail you from your purpose.

As I was writing this book, I had a serious bout of imposter syndrome, resulting in writer's block. I then spoke to a friend, who was also a client, about impostor syndrome getting the best of me. She told me I had something to offer, urged me to take a positive break, and do an enjoyable activity before continuing to write. It was just the encouragement I needed. The antidote to imposter syndrome is to know its foundation is on the fear of not being enough, and its principal aim is to paralyse you from acting. Once you acknowledge this fact, focus on doing what you set out to do, regardless of your fear.

I won't ask syndrome

This syndrome comes from the mistaken belief that we are super(wo)men. It affects men and women equally, but because women have multiple roles in multiple spheres, if they believe they can do it all, all the time, they end up burning out because they consider asking for help as a sign of weakness or worse still, a sign of failure to cope.

The antidote to this barrier is to learn that asking for help multiplies your ability to focus on what matters. Better still, it enables others to feel valuable as they offer you help and their insights.

I can't toot my horn syndrome (false modesty)

False modesty is another saboteur that gets in the way of becoming your next best self especially for women. It is usually founded on cultural norms that are dictated from a patriarchal perspective that women were to be seen not heard. Our work was meant to speak for itself, if at all. This made women never consider tooting their horn. Any woman who spoke about her achievements, or sought a leadership opportunity, was seen as vain and treated with contempt.

However, workplaces and organisations have since evolved, office politics have become more toxic and the fact that opportunities are limited make it an imperative to speak about your achievements in an authentic way that enables you get a chance to make an impact at the next level.

Toxic Comparison

Toxic comparison is the root of most of the sabotaging habits described in this chapter. This is because toxic comparison is founded in negativity and with it comes with its twin habits—envy and jealousy.

Who do you compare yourself with?

When did this start? Perhaps as a child your parents or teachers compared you with others to the point of envy?

It's time to take hold of this self-diminishing habit and choose to focus on becoming your next best self, just as Jordan Peterson says, 'stop comparing yourself with others. Instead compare yourself with who you were yesterday.'

We must always remember that we are the sum total of our experiences and the choices we have made. As you begin your journey to becoming your next best self, it is important to assess your saboteurs so as to overcome them.

BREAKTHROUGH COACHING

1. *Which of the 10 saboteurs discussed is your most toxic one?*

procrastination

false modesty

2. *What is the next step you will take to begin managing this saboteur?*

- Overcome the fear and focus on task

- Share about my dreams + achievements

- Keep good record

Understand and Accept Your Season

> Be yourself—not your idea of what you think somebody else's idea of yourself should be.
>
> ~ **Henry David Thoreau**

'Thank you for hosting this lovely birthday dinner. When you get to a certain age, you stop worrying about what people think. You focus on doing the right thing no matter what. You realise that less is more, and you stop doing things that are incongruent with your life's purpose and values. You focus on faith, family, and meaningful work. That is the power of knowing, accepting, and optimally living in your season.'

These were my older friend Daniella Achieng's words of wisdom as she turned 70.

SEASONS OF TIME

Depending on how old you are, there are specific seasons that align with your age. Let us look at each season:

The Twirling Teens (Ages 11-19)

The teenage years are characterised by dynamic change physically, emotionally, mentally, and socially. Many teenagers struggle with finding and understanding themselves, and use this season as an opportunity to seek and find who they are meant to be, sometimes in the wrong places. When they seek guidance, they discover new ways of understanding, new knowledge, and new peer identity. I call this season twirling teens because the teenagers go round and round in different circles and aspects of their life as they start the journey towards adulthood, and knowing who their next best self appears to look like.

The Try-out Twenty's (Ages 20–29)

I call this period try-out because during this stage, many people have completed their foundational education and may be in tertiary or higher education or entry-level jobs. They are trying out how adult life looks like and do a lot of trial and error during this time, whether in their choice of career, causes they support, or social relational spheres like getting married and starting a family. This trial and error helps them identify what they do not want and what they want.

The Turbulent and Triumphant Thirty's (Ages 30–39)

This season is called turbulent because real adulthood sets in, with responsibilities and clear consequences of one's actions. It is also called triumphant, as it is the season people invest in many firsts. A first home, a first serious job, a first loan or mortgage, a first major decision in their personal or professional life.

These first decisions have a daunting effect on those in this age group because they begin to realise that life is not a rehearsal and should be taken a bit more seriously. They see that any decision they make brings with it some turbulence and some results (triumphs).

The Fortified and Fabulous Forty's (Ages 40–49)

Elements of this season include maturity, a coming of age, and a season of reflection. For many, they feel this is the mid-point in their lives, or as Bob Dunford calls it, half-time. The old adage, life begins at 40, is possibly a combination of societal expectations and previous life expectancy being at 80. Those in season tend to feel the pressure to become their next best self. Many celebrate their 40th birthday and in subsequent years, go through a type of mid-life crisis questioning the meaning of life. They question if they made the right decisions in the previous seasons, and if they can now make life more worthwhile. Because of this crisis, the people one listens to can determine whether an individual will have an upward or downward trajectory for the rest of their life.

The word fortified refers to going through a process of forging what matters and what does not matter; a process of determining your genuine friends and restating what values matter most. This is a season of intense inner growth and where many start to catch up with areas in their lives they had not previously focused on, yet feel matter.

The Flaming Fifty's (Ages 50–59)

The season is called flaming especially because it refers to the menopausal effect women experience in their 50's, when the temperatures swing due to hormonal shifts. Men also go through their own hormonal shifts during this season.

The flaming fifty's are characterised with a coming into one's own. For many in their fifty's, their children have grown and they are anticipating an empty nest season in their marriages after focusing on childbearing and child raising in previous seasons.

For some, they are at the pinnacle of their career, serving on boards and key leadership positions in their areas of influence. Others are running businesses and focusing on impact, significance, and legacy. Many in this season are bold, unapologetic, not influenced by peer pressure, courageous, and with a strong inner ability that is derived from being comfortable in their own skin.

The Sizzling Sixty's (Ages 60–69)

They are sizzling because for those who have made the right choices in previous seasons, they begin to harvest the fruit of their labour. They reinvent themselves and restart their journey of becoming their next best selves with clarity and purpose, based on a spirit of gratitude, knowing that life is finite and not all battles must be fought.

The Serene Seventy's (Ages 70–79)

This is a peaceful season. I have found from my interaction with those in this age bracket, including my parents, they are not frazzled by life's challenges, for they have the gift of perspective. They have deep wisdom based on experience. Many of those in this season are grandparents and relish and enjoy the new role of grandparenthood. Many have had careers, tried multiple businesses, found a rhythm in their retirement, are giving back to their community consistently, and as a result, they are peaceful and serene.

For those of us blessed to have family and friends in this season and beyond, it is the time to document and record through various digital platforms, who they are, what they stood for, what their experiences did to shape them, and what advise they leave for the next generation.

The Unafraid Eighty's (Ages 80–89)

As the word suggests, those in this age bracket are not afraid of anything. Many of them are ready to pass on and meet their Maker, yet they continue to enjoy life to the extent that they can. They speak freely, advise consistently, and are not afraid about what you will think of them. Human respect and playing to the gallery are not traps they fall prey to.

The Noble Ninety's (Ages 90–99)

These are the senior citizens who are called noble because they are a treasure and have blessed those around them with the gift of life and service. Often, they are not able to do many things they were able to do in their past and rely heavily on their family and caregivers. For those who have the gift of taking care of the noble ninety's, consider it a precious gift to be of service to them even if it is not so easy to have a permanent spirit of service and to be at their beck and call.

The Celebratory Hundreds (100 Years and Above)

These individuals are rare. People from different parts of the world like Japan tend to live longer due to lifestyle choices. If you know someone who is in this age bracket, commit to celebrate him or her in all the ways you can. Their life and experiences are a gift to all mankind.

To harness your season, first accept it. Let go of the expectations you had of achieving certain things by a certain age.

Then embrace the benefits of the season. Ensure that you look at your age as a blessing, practise acceptance, and do what you need to do in the season you are in. For my fellow ladies, do not hide your age; by stating how old you are, you exercise courage, confidence, compassion, and gratitude for your season.

THE SEASONS OF PROCESS

Another way to look at seasons, especially in our personal and professional lives, is by using the farming analogy. Farmers must trust the process and honour each season of growth to reap a bountiful harvest.

The season of tilling

This season is about preparing yourself for the steps ahead. You could be learning a skill, or investing in knowledge that will be the base of who you want to be.

A significant tilling season for me was searching for the right school and doctoral program for my interests and circumstances.

The season of planting

This is a season characterised by hard work and long hours even when others may not understand why. It is the season of learning. I am reminded of Cecilia Basigala, who worked by day and studied by night after taking care of her family's needs. Many of her friends asked why she worked so hard with no visible results. Some even taunted her schooling efforts, saying it was in vain. This initially discouraged Cecilia, but she soon recognised the necessary season of planting, thus persisting with courage and focus, and today, she is a proud graduate. After all, FOCUS, as an acronym means: follow one course until successful.

The season of watering

This is a season of nurturing your goal and plan. It is the season where you raise your level of accountability and discipline. This is because you cannot rely solely on the weather to provide the rainwater you need for your seeds to germinate. This is a season of persistence, courage, and hope. Accountability here is important because telling a person you trust about your goal, plan, and progress will enable them to urge you on when you feel discouraged or unwilling to continue working on your goal.

The season of germination

In this season, just like a plant, you begin to see the sprouts of your goals and dreams emerge from the earth.

Loise and John Njoka had been married for a long time and were waiting for the blessing of a child. When the blessing finally came, their season of germination was their season of pregnancy. For a child learning how to speak or an adult learning a new language or skill, this season of germination is akin to when they are able to string a list of words and create a coherent sentence. Germination is a season of new beginnings.

The season of pruning and weeding

This is a painful but necessary season. It is the season of working on those habits that no longer serve you well as you aim to grow. It is the season of auditing your life, your time, your social relationships, the way you use your money and resources, and what you invest in compared to your commitment to become your next best self.

This season is painful because it is a brutally truthful season.

Just like a good farmer will go through his or her garden to check what is ailing the seeds from growing and weed them out, that's the same way we should brutally assess, audit, and call out with authenticity what is ailing our progress. The decision and commitment to root out the weeds is painful, yet, it is the main reason why your goals and plans will grow from strength to strength.

The season of growth

The season of steady growth normally happens if we honour and follow through on what is required of us in the previous seasons. It is the season when you start to see different results from your commitment to your goals and plans. The results may be personal, and only you can see and experience them, or external, where others can see the changes taking place in you as you grow.

The harvesting season

This is the season when the results of your goals and plans become a source of growth for others. Just like a farmer does not harvest the produce for himself, but for his family, community, and customers who will buy his bounty harvest from the marketplace, so does the harvesting season. The growth you have achieved is not just for your enjoyment only, but for others too.

1.   *Which season based on the two analogies discussed are you in?*

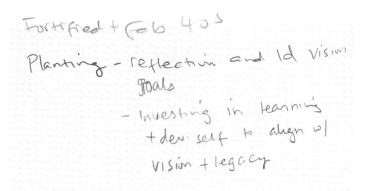

Fortified + Feb 40s

Planting - reflection and ld vision
      goals
      - Investing in learning
      + dev. self to align w/
      vision + legacy

2.   *Do you see any overlaps?*

Yes - esp w/ seasons. s/times
I feel I am in several seasons @
the same time

3.   *What do you commit to do after reading this chapter?*

- Enjoy the season I am @
- Align w/ God plans.

Be Unapologetic About Your Self-care

It takes courage to grow up and become who you really are.

~ **E E Cummings**

'How can this younger generation be so selfish as to make their needs come first? Where did they learn this terrible habit?' This was the agony several older ladies were expressing at a forum I once attended. Unfortunately, many of us confuse self-care with being selfish because culturally and socially, we may have been taught that when you put yourself first, it is selfish and self-centred. Historically in Africa, women took pride in being the last to eat, first to rise, and the last to sleep.

Because of an increase in lifestyle diseases, and in 2020 due to the global pandemic, research by the American Psychological Association (APA) has shown that self-care has never been more important than at this time. We each must metaphorically fill up our cups of self-care as part of becoming our next best selves.

WHAT IS SELF-CARE?

This is the habit of taking care of yourself daily in five different spheres of your life. People relate self-care with selfishness because of the dominant focus on me-time that took centre-stage over the last decade. However, I have found that when you refocus on the intention, and rectify it to invest in self-care so as to serve others better, the guilt associated with self-care is eliminated.

At Breakthrough, we call it the 5-finger self-care goal-setting model inspired by Pope Francis's 5-finger prayer.

The thumb represents physical well-being

Physical well-being relates to your physical state. The state of your health, weight, sleep patterns, and stress management all contribute to your physical well-being.

The index finger represents mental and intellectual well-being

This is your ability to develop your way of thinking, make decisions, and solve problems. Potential ways of developing your mental well-being is by choosing to learn, unlearn, and relearn by reading books and articles wisely, meditating, reflecting, journaling, committing to increase your education and apply the knowledge learnt, and regularly managing your social media.

THE POWER OF UNAPOLOGETIC SELF-CARE

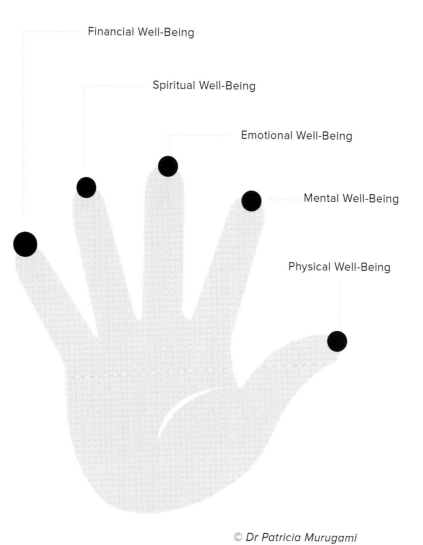

Financial Well-Being

Spiritual Well-Being

Emotional Well-Being

Mental Well-Being

Physical Well-Being

© Dr Patricia Murugami

The middle finger represents emotional well-being

This refers to the state of your emotions. Are you often angry, peaceful, hurt, bitter, happy, serene, grateful, or anxious? Knowing how you feel and what triggers those emotions is important.

I have found if I am perpetually in a negative state of emotions, I may need to dig deep and deal with the issue. If it is something I cannot change, I need to start accepting it. If it is something that continues to hurt me, I need to clean the wound, forgive myself and the other person who is causing me pain.

Whatever the emotion, deal with it and aim to get to a more peaceful state, as our emotions ultimately determine the relationship we have with ourselves and with others.

The fourth finger, also called the ring finger, represents spiritual well-being

This refers to the relationship you have with God. Many people believe in a higher being. We believe in God yet do not cultivate a relationship whereby God can influence our daily life and journey towards becoming our next best self.

Consider getting to know your faith and cultivating a set of daily spiritual habits that include prayer, reading spiritual books, examining your conscience, and other prayers that will form and strengthen your conscience and spiritual life.

The fifth and small finger refers to financial well-being

It is the last goal because all the other fingers and aspects of well-being influence how you develop your financial well-being.

Ways you can develop your financial well-being is to set a budget, spend and save, and to monitor any financial deviations.

When my husband and I went to see a financial coach as part of our financial well-being, the first thing she did was ask us about our relationship with money and what money meant to us from as early as we could remember. She then analysed our money personality and got us to see what triggered our money habits as individuals and as a couple. Finally, she asked us to track for a month every expense we made no matter how small. That was a hard task, requiring daily discipline but at the end of it all, when we looked at our patterns of spending, it was illuminating and enabled us change some of our negative ways and continue some strong money habits we already had.

The thing about self-care is to determine what is your anchor goal. The anchor goal is the area that you consider to be most important for this season and which when you commit to doing, releases energy and impact on the other goals. My anchor goal this year was my spiritual well-being as it is the foundation and well-spring of all the other 4 areas of well-being. For someone else, their anchor goal could be their physical well-being.

REFLECT ON THE 5 FINGERS. DECIDE ON YOUR ANCHOR GOAL.

Then commit to the smallest, tiniest step, which is what I refer to as a micro-habit. Unapologetically begin to execute your the micro-habit. When you start to do this micro-habit consistently, it will enable you achieve your anchor goal and also have a ripple effect on the other four areas of your well-being.

BREAKTHROUGH COACHING

1. *Which is your anchor goal for this season?*

    Spiritual wellbeing

2. *Which micro-habit have you committed to do to achieve your anchor goal?*

    - Quiet time
    - Start early

3. *What is your goal for your physical well-being?*

    Be physically active 30 min a day

4. *What is your plan to achieve this goal?*

    Run
    cycle

5. *What is your goal for your mental-intellectual well-being?*

    - Read - book a month / chap a day
    - listen to podcast

    -

6. *What is your plan to achieve this goal?*

    - listen to podcast
    - Read a book a month

7. *What is your goal for your emotional well-being?*

Be peaceful / @ peace

8. *What is your plan to achieve this goal?*

- Forgive quickly + Completely
- Resolve issues
- Listen + my emotions

9. *What is your goal for your spiritual well-being?*

Establish vision statement

10. *What is your plan to achieve this goal?*

- Reflection, meditation, discerning
- Prayer
- Reading

11. *What is your goal for your financial well-being?*

- Spend less
- Be generous
- establish Cost of living for us. - how much we need

12. *What is your plan to achieve this goal?*

- Stop buying clothes + stuff 2nd yr runnin
- Give more
- Sustain minimalism lifestyle.

How High Is Your
Relational Intelligence?

Because true belonging only happens when
we present our authentic, imperfect selves to
the world, our sense of belonging can never
be greater than our level of self acceptance.

~ **Brené Brown**

» What kind of people do you need for the season you are in?

» What kind of person are you to others?

Kikulacho ki nguoni mwako. This Swahili proverb translates to: that which destroys you is very close to you. I thought this proverb was a cliché until I experienced its meaning. Mwikali Mula was a happy, social and warm person. She was kind-hearted and altruistic, always looking to lift someone's spirits and help them advance. She was also very talented, what is now referred to as being a multipotentialite, and could do many things very well. She run a fast-growing retail business that was expanding across the country and beyond.

Mwikali was loyal, almost to a fault. She believed she had lifelong friends and gave of herself accordingly.

One day, her childhood friend, Munatsya borrowed some money for an urgent need. Mwikali did not think twice even though it was a significant amount she valued her friend and believed they had similar values. She wired the money to Munatsya's account and knew she would return the interest-free loan within one month's time as agreed.

When the month ended, Mwikali, being a lady of her word, expected the same from her friend. Alas, the second month ended and Munatsya did not show any signs of paying. Worse still, they had met socially a number of times, and Munatsya did not even broach the subject. When Mwikali tried calling, Munatsya did not respond.

After suffering a lot of angst and being bewildered as to what was happening, Mwikali sought counsel from Wambui, an older wiser friend and mentor. As Wambui comforted her, she told her a few truths she would never forget:

'Mwikali, not all people you consider to be friends are genuine friends. Not all your friends are celebrating your business growth and stable family. Very few friends can mix business and friendship. Not all people have the pure heart and open uplifting spirit you have. That does not mean you become bitter and selfish. It means you need to raise your boundaries and choose who you trust very wisely. Remember, values are not what people say, but what they do and in many cases, some friends do not have the same values you commit to.'

Mwikali painfully realised she needed to pay more attention to the lessons the wise school of life offered. She courageously faced her friend and confronted her about why she had not honoured her commitment.

Unfortunately, Munatsya opted to be arrogant and Mwikali had to use a legal process to get her money back, and that was the end of that friendship.

To become your next best self, the people you treasure and those who influence you in one way or another have a dramatic effect on you and your ability to grow intentionally.

I have found that there are five types of people you will come across as you relate with others. I use the house analogy to describe them. When you have the right people around you, they help you grow in multiple ways.

FOUNDATION PEOPLE

These people like a house's foundation, are always there for you and have been there for you for as long as you can remember. They anchor you and remind you what matters and the values that make you who you are. They were there from the very start, are kindred spirits, and all-weather people just like a firm foundation.

They do not judge you when you show them your struggles and imperfections. Foundation people wholly accept you for who you are. You may not necessarily talk deeply with these individuals daily, but they influence your daily habits and perspectives. They allow you to stand on their shoulders and encourage you to continue growing, aiming high, and becoming your next best self.

Due to their almost invisible nature, the risk is that we can easily take them for granted. These people are bold with courage and faithful love for you. They will go to war for you because they believe in you and what you stand for. They are never shy to show that you are one of their people. For me, my foundation squad includes my parents, my husband, my children, and some very special friends who have been there in my good times and bad, ready to walk with me through my situations with love, trustworthiness, and commitment.

PILLAR PEOPLE

These are people who support you as you grow just like the pillars in a house. They only show up when you need to grow. They include mentors, coaches, teachers, and loyal friends who are willing to help you fight your current battles and prepare for the proverbial war. They are never embarrassed or judgmental about anything you tell them. They carry your load as if it is theirs. For me, my pillar people continue to be my family members, my accountability mentors, and a few critical friends and teachers.

WALL PEOPLE

These people are there with you for only a season. They usually enjoy the bright seasons of your life and celebrate with you. However, just like walls, they may need high maintenance and investment. They may protect you for a season, but just like walls, need regular wiping, painting, and maintenance. When seasons change, like walls, they may crack and let you down in your hour of need. Be careful of wall people but at the same time, be grateful for the season they are in your life.

WINDOW PEOPLE

These are very high maintenance type of people and tend to be there for a reason. Just like the windows in our homes, they need to be cleaned often and covered by curtains. They shine when the sun is shining and are dull when things are not going well.

Window people are fair-weather friends who are only there when things are going well. They tend to be fragile and may not withstand the storms and hurricanes of life, as their focus is to make progress on mutual goals. Window people could include classmates or work and business colleagues who connect with you because you are in the same class or work space.

ROOF PEOPLE

Just like a roof, these individuals, visible from the outside, are in your life for a reason. You may not know them deeply and they serve a specific purpose. Roof people are acquaintances who may know what you are doing, leadership sponsors who cheer you on, serve as a reference, critique your work, and generally shield you from a far.

BREAKTHROUGH COACHING

1. *Who are your foundation people?*

   - Liz
   - Mercy
   - parents
   - Cero

2. *Who are your pillar people?*

   - Zippy, Princesses
   - Chapel - Mary wamae   Sophy, Lindua
              - Bea + Oscar
              - Shiru
   Mr mugambi, mrs omoto, mrs mhno, mrs Gikonyo

3. *Who are your wall people?*

   Esther adhiambo
   caro mus
   Friends quero

4. *Who are your window people?*

   Workmates
   Campo BS

5. *Who are your roof people?*

   BS grp

6. *What kind of person are you to the people you treasure?*

   pillar to the dream s/times I am wall/window

7. *What do you commit to do after reading this chapter?*

   Be a pillar to others
   Be foundation for my fam
   Roof

Confront and Forgive Yourself for Your Dark Side

> To thine own self be true.
>
> ~ **Shakespeare**

When I was younger, I was what you can call an extreme optimist until life taught me to be a realistic optimist. I learnt the hard way as a teenager, that I had an excessive need for belonging. There was a peer group I really wanted to be part of but they made it clear I did not meet their criteria. However, my need for belonging and optimism kept me insisting and trying to fit in by doing things that were contrary to who I was. Sadly, I never belonged and it took one betrayal to know it was time to let go of that need.

Each of us has a dark side. We all have lights and shadows to our character. It is about what drives us more regularly: is it our light or dark side? Our needs and values determine the side that becomes prominent.

Here are some key needs that can excessively drive a human being regardless of their status and position in life:

1. Excessive need for belonging

   You want to be part of a group of people at any cost.

2. Excessive need to please

   You want people to be happy with what you do and to tell you they are. You crave for acceptance and can easily become a people pleaser.

3. Excessive need for control

   You want people to do things only your way and when they don't, you get angry and demand that they abide by your rules. As a result, people around you tend to stop thinking and sharing new ideas that could mutually benefit you and them.

4. Excessive need for information

   You always want to know it all, no matter how high the cost of getting that information is, you are willing to betray trust and break confidences to get it.

5. Excessive need for recognition

   You crave recognition for all the work you do and the achievements you attain. As a result, you continue to be held at the mercy of other people noticing and validating your achievements. If they do not recognise you, you feel worthless.

6. **Excessive need for approval**

You cannot make a decision without getting people's approval that you are on the right track. Without that approval, you are unable to make decisions and act on them in a mature way.

7. **Excessive need for appreciation**

You cannot feel fulfilled until others appreciate you. Your own internal appreciation that you have done your best is not enough for you until others applaud and appreciate you.

The risk of being driven by these needs is that you are held hostage to your most dominant needs if they are not met.

Once you know your highest excessive need, it is time to confront it and forgive yourself for chasing after a need in a way that did not serve you well. Forgive yourself, but do not forget the lesson, as you become your next best self.

BREAKTHROUGH COACHING

1. Rank the needs we have discussed beginning with your current highest need.

    7, 5, 3

2. Think about the last time you felt deeply disappointed, which need had not been met?

    7+5   appreciation + recognition

3. How else can you meet that need?

    Blow my trumpet ☺

    - Treat myself
    - make a list of ways I have impressed myself

4. What will it take to let go of that need?

    Remember whose I am and who I am

5. What do your commit to do after reading this chapter?

    understand my self better

THE
SECOND LEVEL

The Power of Raising Your Head

aising your head entails raising your mind and intellectual abilities to solve a life or leadership challenge while sharpening your skills and leadership ability. Raising the head means applying effort to gain knowledge, which you can then convert into actions. When you repeat actions consistently, they form habits that become part of your authentic character. Raising your head will move you from the state of not knowing to competence (knowing) as you continue becoming the person you were created to be; your next best self.

- vision
- Identity
- Competence
- Values
- Influence

What Is Your VUCA Vision?

" "

A vision is not just a picture of what could be; it is an appeal to our better selves' a call to become something more.

~ **Rosabeth Moss Kanter**

2020. History in the making or is it unmaking?

It was an unprecedented leap year. I remember starting the year with such anticipation, hitting the ground running and getting on with the business of achieving my personal, family, and business vision. Then COVID-19 hit the globe, and with it went many visions as it threw all plans into disarray.

But unknown to me, the visions I had thought and written down were to be disrupted, yet the intention remained the same. What do I mean? Interestingly, in 2019, one of our Breakthrough goals was to go global and help many more people breakthrough their challenges to become their next best selves.

» 2020 forced us to go global faster, and in ways we had not thought about.

» 2020 forced us to take a giant pause, reset and rethink our priorities.

» 2020 forced us to know that less is more.

» 2020 forced us to recalibrate what matters.

» 2020 taught us to be more grateful.

» 2020 taught us to intentionally evaluate our values and live them in action.

» 2020. The leap year that got us rethinking our vision, values and who we really are.

2020 inspired me to think about VUCA differently. In the midst of the pain, struggles, dark and light times, a new idea was formed. My original vision had to morph into something else, yet the power of a vision is that it keeps you focused and hopeful in a certain direction, even when the season seems so bleak.

VUCA Rebranded

I regularly taught the acronym VUCA as Volatile, Uncertain, Complex, and Ambiguous times.

2020 did not even begin to meet this definition. It has been an outlier on many fronts. So, I decided it was time to rethink this VUCA acronym so that I could help others have a brighter outlook and breakthrough their crises.

After many hours of reflection I developed the new VUCA that enables us weather any storm and become our next best selves.

V refers to our ability to **visualise** a brighter future.

U refers to our ability to **unlearn** habits and attitudes that no longer serve us well and that get in the way of actualising your vision.

C refers to **creatively** learning that which helps us navigate today better and achieve our vision more effectively.

A refers to **agile adaptability,** that is, the decisions you make and implement with flexibility to adapt to the new circumstances in your life and achieve your vision.

THE BREAKTHROUGH VUCA MODEL

© *Dr Patricia Murugami*

What you can't visualise, you can't see. What you can't see, you can't become.

BREAKTHROUGH COACHING

1. Take time to reflect on your dreams and vision for yourself, your family, and your team.

2. When did you last dream of a better future ahead?

3. When did you last allow yourself to visualise your next best self?

4. What do you want to visualise for yourself, your family, your team?

5. What do you need to unlearn?

   - Unforgiveness
   - Dealing w/ 4th space
   - Procastination - Sloth tendancies

6. What do you need to creatively learn?

   - know myself and be peaceful
   - Reflect God's love in my life
   - speak w/ Clarity + wisdom

7. What do you commit to do after reading this VUCA chapter?

   - Spend quality time w/ God, fam, friends
   - Invest in self dev - read, reflective practice

Give Yourself Permission to Become a Beginner

The illiterate of the 21st century will not be those who cannot read and write, but those who cannot learn, unlearn, and relearn.

~ **Alvin Toffler**

When I completed my Doctorate in Business Administration, in the midst of multiple celebrations, a mentor reminded me something worth sharing. She said, 'No matter how high we climb up, we will always be at the beginning and bottom of the next mountain.'

That grounded me instantly and out of that experience, I realised the importance of having a kindergarten child's mind-set even if I was at the top pinnacle of education having completed a doctorate degree.

THREE TYPES OF LEARNERS

In my decades of leadership development and coaching experience, in previous academic institutions and now at Breakthrough, I have narrowed down the types of learners who walk into the classes and coaching sessions we conduct into three groups:

The spectator learner

This person goes through life watching others, complaining and opting to do the bare minimum when it comes to learning and growing. They watch others in the learning experience without any intentional engagement or learning objective. They only want to rest and recuperate from life's stresses.

The victim learner

This person has been pushed to the learning experience by their boss or other external forces. They would rather not be there and are absent from the entire learning opportunity. They opt in many cases to be disruptive and have a critical spirit, distracting others from learning and growing. This person has a victim mentality.

The intentional learner

This is the person who is ready to grow. They are ready to moult their proverbial old skin and grow into a better version of themselves. This person may have been beaten by life's storms and is looking for a solution. This person has received feedback and knows something has to give. They are searching deeply for a way to reinvent themselves. This person, consciously or sub-consciously is looking for a way to become their next best self.

I hope you are an intentional learner. And if by any chance you were forced to read this book, and started reading it as a victim or spectator, I hope you are now convinced about the importance of transitioning to become an intentional learner.

Being an intentional learner is not only for a formal class setting, it should also be applicable to your entire life. This is the advantage of a beginner's mind-set, which never thinks that the value and knowledge one has is enough. After all, they say that when we stop learning, that is when we start dying.

What are the characteristics of an intentional learner?

» An intentional learner is curious.

» An intentional learner is open to learning from what seem to be apparent failures.

» An intentional learner does not discriminate who he or she learns from. This learner knows that the teachers of life's lessons come in many forms.

» An intentional learner is not afraid to ask for help or seek clarification.

» An intentional learner is not afraid to course correct when they learn something new.

» An intentional learner is not afraid to share his or her ideas and experiences.

BREAKTHROUGH COACHING

1. *In the school of life, which of these three learners are you currently?*

   Intentional

2. *What caused you to become that learner?*

   - Reflective journey 45 days to 45
   - Covid 19 / lock down

3. *What do you commit to do after reading this chapter?*

   Sustain curiosity and be open t
   learn from God + others.

   Explore innovation

Your Identity Is More Than Your Job

The privilege of a lifetime is to become who you truly are.

~ **Carl Jung**

Michelle Young had taken a career break to nurture her young family and was now contemplating re-entry into the workplace. But she had serious doubts as to whether she was worthy or experienced enough.

When she came in for her first coaching session, I asked her to describe what she had been doing over the last 6 years. She began to list the things she did to nurture and develop the character of her children, managing the family finances, real estate projects, resolving conflicts, and dealing with different challenges in the family.

I then asked her to rebrand those activities into corporate jargon. This is how we began:

- » We changed nurturing and developing the character of her children to talent acquisition and development.
- » Managing the family finances to financial management.
- » Real estate projects to project management and estate planning.
- » Resolving conflicts to emotional intelligence and conflict resolution

As she spoke, renamed and rebranded the tasks, her posture straightened up, she began glowing with confidence and had clarity of focus on how she would prepare her profile, introduction, and presentation.

I urged her on by telling her that there was no one who has ever put a price or salary on the work of a house wife and stay-at-home mum because her work is invaluable and that should fill her with pride and courage despite the raging comparisons made by women who work out of the home. I reminded Michelle, that we are each the sum total of all our experiences, choices, and lessons learnt.

As such, our identity is much more than our job.

Who are you stripped of your titles, accolades, and achievements?

During a training event many years ago, a facilitator asked us to introduce ourselves without our titles.

We were all struggling to think about who we were beyond our jobs. This was especially difficult since at the time, I was working with a big brand and found that the brand lent a larger- than-life aura to my life. As I struggled to introduce myself, I quickly realised that this was a negative narrative I was developing.

I needed to expand who I was by paying more attention to other things besides work.

Who are you without your paid job?

I have read and heard that for some people, especially men, when they are retrenched or retired, if they had not thought about the answer to this question, deteriorate, get sick and in some cases, pass on due to the lack of identity, structure, and the emptiness they experience without their previous job.

You can change the narrative by committing to develop your identity beyond your professional role. Did you know you have an intrinsic power to grow and become your next best self? And that only you can make that decision and commit to it? Did you also know that you cannot change anyone else?

not your husband,

not your wife,

not your children,

not your in-laws,

not your parents,

not your siblings

not to your colleagues,

not your boss,

not your friends,

not your neighbours,

not your business partners,

not your entire social ecosystem of people who you know.

Only you can choose to do something about how you think, feel, act, become, and develop your identity.

Remember, emotional intelligence teaches that where you focus and allocate your energy is where you will get the highest return on investment. And by extension, you may find your social ecosystem starts to change because of the power of your example.

What narrative are you telling yourself and others?

BREAKTHROUGH COACHING

1. Who are you stripped of your titles?

Woman of God — Photographer
Mother — Traveller
wife
Friend
Comm. leader
encourager

2. How do your professional life and skills develop your personal skills?

— conferencing
- Analysing info / data
- planning / Strategies
- managing
- report writing

3. Which of the two spheres of your life do you identify more with? Why?

work because Its valued more in soc.
- brings money, measurable

4. What do you commit to do to develop your identity beyond your job?

- Engage in other activities beyond work
- Introduce myself in non work identity
yes

Raise Your Competence

Leaders who don't read cannot lead
with impact in these dynamic times.

~ **Patricia Murugami**

'That leader is incompetent! He doesn't know what he doesn't know and pretends to know it all.' I gasped inwardly as I heard the inept description of one manager during a board meeting. I felt sorry that a key decision was being made about his future based on his perceived level of competence.

How competent are you?

This is not a trick question.

It does not require you to speak about the school you went to and the grades or qualifications you got then.

According to Harvard Business Review, any first degree a person gets is obsolete after five years due to the rapid change of the environment. Thus, your ability to exercise agility and raise your ability to grow is what matters, when you talk about competence.

Raising your competence

Competence is a combination of learning agility, skills, and attitude. But competence only matters if it's anchor and intention is solving a problem.

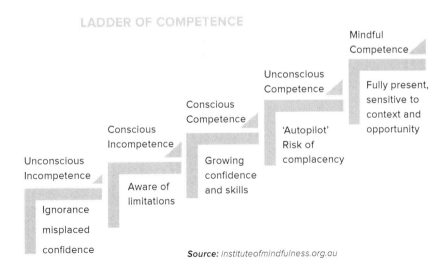

LADDER OF COMPETENCE

Mindful Competence

Unconscious Competence

Conscious Competence

Conscious Incompetence

Unconscious Incompetence

Ignorance misplaced confidence

Aware of limitations

Growing confidence and skills

'Autopilot' Risk of complacency

Fully present, sensitive to context and opportunity

Source: *instituteofmindfulness.org.au*

There are 5 levels of competence growth according to Amy E. Seymour-Walsh in her Theory of Learning.

Unconscious incompetence

This is the learning space where we do not know what we don't know. This is also known as ignorance. Sometimes we do not know the perceived and actual effect of some of our decisions and actions. Other times, we learn how to reduce this knowledge gap by seeking genuine constructive feedback, humbly accepting it and acting on it to improve. Learning in this phase can be painful and discouraging but brings immense insights and wisdom when taken with a growth mind-set.

Conscious incompetence

This is the learning space where we know what we do not know and have to apply our mind consciously to what we are learning. This is driven by the curious quest to know more. This realisation and motivation for curious growth comes through training, assessments, reflection and feedback.

This is where aha moments occur when we realise that we have learnt something deeply and in a way that helps us close this gap.

Conscious competence

This is the learning phase where we know what we know, and tend to be proud of this knowledge as it is part of our identity.

This phase tends to be one of confidence and if we are humble, we can teach others what we know. It is also a phase on intentionally gaining more knowledge to perform better in our chosen fields.

Unconscious competence

This is the learning space where we know what we know so well that it is automatic. We can then do it subconsciously without applying too much thought to it as we have excelled in it. This can be likened to what people like to sometimes quip that they can drive home without being fully conscious of the road home as they have driven on it so many times.

The risk is of doing things in autopilot mode is that we can give in to complacency and boredom. An additional risk is that we can become oblivious to changing aspects in the environment especially now as the environment is becoming rapidly dynamic.

Mindful competence

This is the phase where we are aware of our competence areas as we have developed mastery and we are also aware of the dynamic changes in the environment. This phase is characterised with learning agility, which is founded in humility.

To navigate through the competence ladder, we need learning agility based in a beginner's mindset. Learning agility was established in a model designed by researcher Scott DeRue at the University of Michigan that identifies speed and flexibility as the two most important factors determining learning agility. Learning agility is how one can assimilate and understand large data with speed and discern the most important aspects. The ability to be dynamic and change mental learning methods while seeing patterns and sense making to see how unrelated things are connected is learning agility.

GAUGING YOUR LEARNING AGILITY

These questions can help you gauge your learning agility:

When is the last time I learnt something on-the-go? How was the experience?

When is the last time I challenged my status quo and my beliefs about a situation? What did I learn?

How many books have I read this year compared to the number I intend to read? on track for a book a month

What do I intend to learn intentionally for this season? - visuals - plan strategy

How do I learn best? Watching, reading - visual Goal sett'

How about your professional expertise?

» Have you checked if a robot is likely to take over your job?

» How future- ready are you for the work of the future?

» What new skills do you need to learn? - leadership
 - agile learner

» Which old skills do you need to unlearn? work spaces

» Have you assessed your attitude?

» What do you consider to be a positive growth mind-set? - curious
 - ready to learn

» Are you able to reframe any challenge into an opportunity or are you a gloom dispenser who is always pessimistic about the future? s/times

» Do you have regular assessments that enable you see where you are on the ladder of competence?
 not really - Set · quarterly reviews.

BREAKTHROUGH COACHING

1. *What phase of competence are you in your personal life?*

    Conscious Competence

2. *What phase of competence are you in your professional life?*

    unconcious Competence →7 mindfll Competence

3. *What is one thing you commit to do after reading this chapter?*

    Set up quarterly Competence reviews.

Focus on Your Circle of Influence

Don't raise your voice, instead raise the quality of your argument.

~ **Grant Thornton**

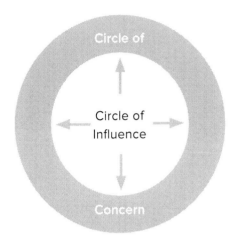

Proactive Focus

*Positive energy
enlarges Circle of
Influence*

Reactive Focus

*Negative energy
reduces Circle of
Influence*

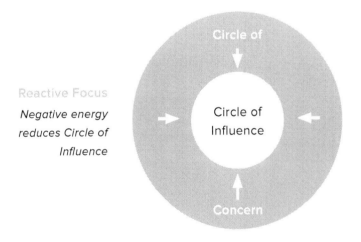

*Source: https://dplearningzone.the-dp.
co.uk/2015/06/24/coveys-circles-of-influence/*

Salome Nikot started feeling unsettled when she was in her first job after graduating from university. She had these sobering thoughts about the meaning of life and what she was supposed to do with her life. As she started her research job, she was open to learning all she could but at the end of the day, Salome felt empty.

Over lunch, she would convene with other colleagues and they would bemoan their life's trajectory, discuss the negative politics of the day, the life-altering climate change and other company, national, and global issues. After lunch, Salome would always feel defeated and discouraged.

Then one day, she read a book about a renowned female scientist and realised that the force driving their groundbreaking work was solving a problem she was passionate about by focusing on what she could do about it.

Salome decided to take time to reflect on the problems she was passionate about and focused her attention on discovering more about these problems. She even challenged her colleagues over lunch to rethink their conversations and focus on that which they could do something about. Unbeknownst to her, Salome had started focusing on her circle of influence and in a short time, her level of interest, contribution, and fulfilment shot up.

Stephen Covey introduced this idea in his book *7 Habits of Highly Effective People*. He argues that focusing on your sphere of influence is more effective than on your sphere of concern.

Many of us prefer to discuss issues that annoy or aggrieve us. Whether we find solutions or not is usually not the focus for many of us. Instead, we meet up with colleagues and peers, and spend endless hours on conversations that leave us dissipated and empty. For many people, this is the story of their lives. But, it does not have to be your chosen narrative. The temptation to discuss what's not working, blame others, or berate them is a way of absolving ourselves of any blame or responsibility. However, this just pushes us to be victim learners as we saw earlier.

Commit to shift from discussions that only focus on problems and instead tilt the conversation to seeking solutions and problem-solving.

WHAT IS IN THE CIRCLE OF CONCERN?

The circle of concern consists of things at a macro level that are outside of your control. These could include inflation, political environments, and climate change, all driven by other people's behaviour, beliefs, attitudes, and actions. Most people prefer to focus on what others are not doing, and sadly, they don't take responsibility, grow, and intentionally become their next best selves.

WHAT IS IN THE CIRCLE OF INFLUENCE?

The circle of influence entails all that is within your control and which you can influence. It takes courage to focus on this circle.

Commit intentionally to focus on your circle of influence and make decisions that you can follow through on and impact with a solution to the problem.

As I reflect on my upbringing, my dad would always tell me to focus on my proposed solutions instead of getting worked up. He would paraphrase the quote that started this chapter and continue to ask me to raise the quality of my solutions and see my circle of influence expand.

BREAKTHROUGH COACHING

1. *What have you been focusing on over the last week?*

    ① Friendship, rest
    ② Afghan situation
    ③ Broken world- covid, earthquate, Migrant crossing
         Refugees

2. *Next to each item, indicate whether it is in your circle of concern (CoC) or circle of influence (CoI)*

    ① - CoI
    ②
    ③ 7 CoC

3. *With what you know now, what do you want to focus on?*

    focus on   friendship + rest
        Broken world- pray

4. *What do you commit to do after reading this chapter?*

    Be prayer and seek God's guidance
    on what I can do

Match Your Commitments to Your Values

> Show me your diary and how you spend your money, and I will show you who you are and what you value.
>
> ~ **Patricia Murugami**

Deborah Johnson, a seasoned leader, signed up for an executive coaching session and was asked by her coach to assess her work and life diary and show how she had spent her time over the last month.

Then she was asked to show how she had spent her money over the same period.

When Deborah showed her coach her analysis, she realised that the way she spent her time and money was a reflection of her commitment to her convictions. She was not impressed with how her commitments did not match the values and convictions she had. Worse still, she thought her values were very important, yet, she was not demonstrating them through her chosen actions. After dealing with the initial shock, guilt, and shame, Deborah left that coaching session with a road map on how she would course correct to ensure she was living a more congruent life.

Matching commitments to your values is a process that requires you to be brutally honest. Especially in current times where playing to the gallery is more important for many compared to what we do in secret.

Most people will do whatever it takes to appear to the public in a way that is not honest or linked to their values. This is adult peer pressure and I have found it is more dangerous than teenage peer pressure. So, where do you begin to get this inner alignment?

» Reflect on your last month, what thoughts have been dominant in your life? Are they about making ends meet, money accumulation, impacting others, competing with others, innovative ideas, family, virtues, vices or what?

» Assess where you have spent your time over the last month, account for each minute of your day. Then analyse where your gift of time is going.

» Determine where you have spent your emotions, that is, who has preoccupied your heart? What emotions have you experienced? Is it anger, pain, hurt, joy, frustration, regret, shame, excitement, peace or any other form of emotion?

» Check who you have spent your time with. This is usually a clear reflection of who matters to you.

» Check what habits have featured dominantly during your last month. The tiniest habits done repeatedly form our character...or lack of it (unfortunately).

» Analyse where you have spent your prayer intentions, if you believe in God. What you have been praying for or thanking Him for?

» Finally, check how you have spent your money. Track each and every coin you spend during that month. Analyse what you spent your money on and what this reveals.

» Try and do the above steps over a longer period of time to see what the longer-term effect looks like.

» Write down the values that are coming through—-those are the real values that mean something to you.

» Do you like what you are seeing? If not, commit to change one dimension at a time, start with how you are spending your energy; it has a direct effect on how you spend your time.

Where you spend your time, energy, thought capital, money, and prayers will show you what you authentically value not what you say you value.

Breakthrough Coaching

1. Do the above values exercise and document what you have observed.

2. What values did you think you had?

3. What values have you found out you have from the exercises in this section?

4. What do you commit to do as a result of reading this chapter?

What's On Your 'Stop Doing' List?

> Only the disciplined ones in life are free. If you are undisciplined, you are a slave to your moods and your passions.
>
> ~ **Eliud Kipchoge**

Josephine Kamau was a highly efficient leader who took pride in getting things done and ticking them off her to-do list. She had developed a continuous to-do list that by the time she was halfway through the year, her to-do list was at number 1,057. Who wouldn't panic at having such a to-do list?

One day, on the verge of a burnout, Josephine realised that her to-do list was endless and that she needed to rein it in. But where would she start? Josephine discovered she needed to stop doing certain things so as to create the mental space, emotional bandwidth, and energy to focus on what truly mattered and to be more effective rather than efficient. She then developed her 'stop doing' list and top on the list was to stop saying yes to all the requests made on her time and expertise. By choosing to do this one thing, say a thoughtful no, she freed herself to focus on what was important and became more effective and mindful. For others, maybe we need to say an intentional yes if we are always saying no to opportunities.

Many times we focus on our to-do list. Today, I want to encourage you to instead focus on your 'stop doing' list. This list will help you stop getting in your own way, and move you towards becoming your next best self.

What is a 'stop doing' list?

This is a list of not more than three items that you can create based on habits that are blocking you from becoming your next best self.

These habits rob you of your peace and focus, they distract you, cause you not be a finisher, and drift you far away from who you were created to be.

Examples of a 'stop doing' list

» **Stop keeping the company of toxic friends**: first, they are not really true friends. Friends who gossip, compete with you, are never happy for you when you grow, constantly fill you with self-doubt, and who cause you to move backwards in your life unknowingly, are toxic friends.

» **Stop procrastinating**: Bishop Rosie wrote that procrastination is delaying what you should do with the assumption that God has given you more time to do it. Ouch! That hurt because I have suffered from procrastination. Brian Tracy suggests in his book, *Eat the Frog,* we should start the day with the most impactful task that requires our highest energy, that is, the task we find the hardest. Saint Josemaria Escriva in his book, *The Way* advises that when you conquer the first battle in the day by waking up on time, you will be well ahead for the rest of the day, and this consistent practice develops your fortitude and character.

In other words, don't press snooze ladies and gentlemen, because as they say, when you snooze, you lose. Many of us snooze the first few minutes of the day and as a result, we actually start the day on a losing streak, chasing the lost time from the word go.

Think about those things you've been saying you're going to do: order your drawers, finish that assignment, call someone, meet the deadline, finish your learning program, have a courageous conversation, raise a boundary that is long overdue, and other priorities. Choose to focus on these things and do the things that matter earlier in the day when you have higher energy.

» **Stop ignoring your interior life:** many people struggle to pay attention to their interior life, what I have referred to here as life's whispers. They don't listen to their conscience and as a result, they don't trust their instinct and gut. Many of us have the gift of hindsight, where we see life's lessons after the fact. However, some people have the gift of foresight, where they see the lessons on life emerging in the future. However, they sometimes don't trust their gut and ignore certain signs because they don't think deeply about them.

» **Stop one sabotaging habit**: look back to the chapter where we assessed saboteurs. Select the one that had the most negative effect on you and put it on your 'stop doing' list.

» **Stop saying yes to the approval addiction**: many of us have what Joyce Meyer calls approval addiction in her book *Approval Fix.* We have this disease to please everyone because we somehow think pleasing people will make us feel worthy and valued. We have this phobia that we don't want to be disliked or criticised. Ladies and gentlemen, you need to look this disease to please right in the face and ask yourself, who are these people I'm constantly trying to please?

My parents always told us that the only person we should be afraid of not pleasing, is God: others are independent spectators. Some of them are hoping you will trip and fall, don't worry about those; worry about where your values and virtues are anchored. And never worry about if they will talk, as they will always talk, whether you worry about it or not.

» **Stop comparing yourself with others**: no one can be you. Oscar Wilde said: be yourself, everyone is taken. I want to encourage you, stop comparing yourself with other people; instead, choose to compare yourself with who you were yesterday. I have found that actually choosing to ensure you only spend minimum time on specific social media platforms, which sometimes cause you to compare yourself negatively with others, and to actually think that your life is not really that meaningful (and this advise is not only to teenagers), is very helpful. I think that adults, parents, people in their 30s and 40s struggle with this comparison. People compare themselves based on the stuff they own, the places they live, people they associate with, but frankly, all that is vanity as the Good Book says. I want to encourage you to stop comparing yourself with others, as it will do you no good. You will lose your peace and actually, it will corrode your self-belief and erode your energy to focus on becoming your next best self.

» **Stop that critical spirit:** this critical spirit usually comes from high perfectionistic tendencies. This is where many of us are constantly assessing ourselves against a moving target. You see, when they say that perfectionism is the highest form of self-abuse, it is true. Because when you're a perfectionist, you are never satisfied, you're always thinking about the things that didn't go well, you always drive your team up the wall because nothing is good enough.

I know you probably have many other things to put on your 'stop doing' list, but I believe you should examine yourself today, and check whether you're suffering from the disease to please, whether you're comparing yourself unnecessarily, or procrastinating on critical objectives, tasks, and goals, and whether you have an extremely critical spirit, first towards yourself and then towards others.

Once you examine yourself, write one thing you want to put on your 'stop doing' list. One way to 'stop doing' is to actually replace that negative habit with a positive one. This week, I encourage you not to look at your to-do list, instead focus on your 'stop doing' list; you will be making the steps towards becoming your next best self.

BREAKTHROUGH COACHING

1. *What will you put on your 'stop doing' list?*

   - procastineting
   - fear
   - approval train

2. *How will stopping this habit help you get closer to your next best self?*

   get things done by doing them

3. *What do you commit to do after reading this chapter?*

   Stick to a realistic to do list

Dress How You Want to Be Addressed

Dressing well is a form of good manners.

~ **Tom Ford**

During a group mentoring session, I used the story of Muhammed Ali in the book, *More Than A Hero: Muhammad Ali's Life Lessons Through His Daughter's Eyes,* to explain the concept of dressing the way you want to be addressed:

> 'The chauffeur escorted my younger sister, Laila, and me up to my father's suite. As usual, he was hiding behind the door waiting to scare us. We exchanged many hugs and kisses as we could possibly give in one day. My father took a good look at us, and how we were dressed, sat me down on his lap and said something that I will never forget. 'Hana, everything that God made valuable in the world is covered and hard to get to. Where do you find diamonds? Deep down in the ground covered and protected. Where do you find pearls? Deep down at the bottom of the ocean covered up and protected in a beautiful shell. Where do you find gold? Way down in the mine, covered over with layers and layers of rock. You've got to work hard to get to them.' He looked at me with serious eyes. 'Your body is sacred. You're far more precious than diamonds and pearls, and you should be covered too.'

The lesson hit home for my mentees as it did for Hana.

HOW DO YOU WANT TO BE ADDRESSED?

Many times, we do not realise that how we carry ourselves and how we dress influences our ability to excel in our next opportunity more than how well we have developed our skills for the next level.

For you my sister who is reading this book, how do you want to be addressed?

For you my brother who is reading this book, how do you want to be addressed?

Once you are clear on how your next best self is going to be in terms of character and virtues, then think about how you will dress.

Dressing is a private choice with public consequence. How we dress is also a language to the world in words unspoken except in how we look and act. Choose to audit your wardrobe and weed out what no longer serves you well for the season you are in. It is wiser to invest in a small capsule wardrobe than a bloated wardrobe where you only wear less than 25% of the clothes.

I have had to do a wardrobe audit many times over the years and these three questions always help me make better decisions.

1. Does this item of clothing fit me well now?
2. Does this item reflect my next best self?
3. Is the item in a good state or condition?

If any item gets a no, then it must leave my wardrobe.

You could also consider hiring an image consultant to help you develop your appearance in alignment to your next best self.

For the ladies:

» Develop your personal style that is authentic, classy, elegant and is appropriate to your season and goals.

» Avoid revealing too much and wearing tight clothes. Mystery is the mark of style. We don't need to flaunt everything to feel beautiful.

» Invest in good foundation garments as these provide comfort and confidence.

» Check whether your work clothes demonstrate your competence and ability to solve the business problems. I have served on too many panels to note that sometimes people do not know that their dressing prevents them from being viewed as a capable professional.

» Learn to wear appropriate makeup to accentuate your natural beauty and hide your flaws. Makeup should not alter and mask your beauty.

- » Use colours to your advantage when selecting clothes.

- » Accessorise wisely.

- » Respect the dress code—know the environment you are going to and dress suitably.

- » Take your self-care seriously as inner well-being and beauty radiates on the outside.

- » Be open to feedback and growth and help another person with your sincere compliments and kind critique.

For the gentlemen:

- » Build a solid timeless wardrobe.

- » Invest in developing your personal style.

- » Avoid fads and invest in timeless items.

- » Respect the dress code.

- » Know how to tie a tie well.

- » Invest in at least one black suit that will serve you for formal events.

- » Check your personal grooming and etiquette.

- » Consistently focus on personal hygiene.

- » Ensure your clothes fit well—not too tight or too loose.

- » Guard your intimacy —for instance avoid sagging trousers.

- » Make an effort daily, don't give in to not bothering

- » Be open to feedback and growth and help another person with your sincere compliment and kind critique.

BREAKTHROUGH COACHING

1. *What will you do to dress how you want to be addressed?*

2. *What do you commit to do as a result of reading this chapter?*

Declutter.

The Third Level

The Power of Raising Your Hand and With Your Other Hand, Lift Others

Raising your hand entails, contributing one's talents, knowledge, time and resources for others. It also includes raising your hand to query and fully understand the knowledge at hand. It includes looking for mentors and allowing these mentors to enlighten you in your area of interest by having a coachable and teachable spirit. It requires us to be wisely vulnerable.

Raising your hand is two-fold, it is enabling yourself to lead at the table, accessing leadership opportunities without fear, but also enabling others who do not have a similar opportunity to be mentored and exposed to these opportunities.

When you raise your hand to grasp the next rung in the ladder, the other hand should be free to lift another person who is seeking to rise.

We cannot be people who hold onto the ladder with both hands and worse still when we get to the top, we then drop off the ladder from the wall to ensure nobody else climbs up the leadership ladder. We also cannot be people who break the rungs in the ladder to prevent those behind us from climbing up. That is not leadership.

If Opportunity Does Not Knock, Build a Revolving Door

> The greatest danger for most of us is not that our aim is too high, and we miss it, but that it is too low, and we reach it.
>
> ~ **Michelangelo**

Gladys Kiptum was an upcoming leader in the tech-space, aiming to lead her team to greater heights. One day, she was presented with a big proposal and a very short time limit. She knew from experience that there was no way they could meet the deadline. However, she also knew that this could be her ticket to the next level of leadership so she said yes with no disclaimer. Forty-eight hours later when the proposal was due, she was at her wits end, barking orders to her team and being completely out of character. Needless to say, they did not meet the deadline and she was blamed for being unprepared to lead in turbulence and high-pressure environments. And with that, went her prospects of the promotion and rising to have an impact.

There are many barriers to growth that human beings experience when they are a minority in a professional and leadership environment. These barriers, just like Gladys experienced, cause many to become discouraged and unable to move forward. Let us examine the growing list of opportunity blockers and how you can then build a door that revolves to allow not only yourself in, but others too.

GLASS CLIFF SYNDROME

In 2005, the British Journal of Management published research about the 'glass cliff'. This is when women are given more senior or chief executive roles, but they are roles that men may not be willing to take on, like those with higher potential risk of failure. Thus, the female leader is being set up to fail even before commencing the assignment.

GLASS CEILING

Gay Bryant, who at the time was the editor of Working Woman magazine, first used the phrase glass ceiling in a 1984 Adweek profile. In 1986 the Wall Street Journal's Carol Hymowitz and Timothy Schellhardt popularised the phrase. The glass ceiling syndrome is used to represent an invisible barrier that keeps a given demographic (typically applied to minorities) from rising beyond a certain level in a hierarchy. The metaphor was made in reference to barriers in the careers of high-achieving women. It explains the inability of many women to advance past a certain point in their occupations and professions, regardless of their qualifications or achievements.

GLASS ELEVATOR

Contrary to women, men in female-dominated jobs benefit from a so-called glass elevator or glass escalator, that is, a set of invisible factors that facilitate their professional advancement. New York Times first mentioned this phenomenon, which was then studied at American University's Kogod School of Management. The glass escalator or elevator refers to the fact that men are entering work sectors more 'traditionally' dominated by women—nursing, teaching, administration—and are promoted more quickly than women, creating the effect that they are gliding past women as if on an escalator.

The analysis, based on research by Professor Caren Goldberg at the American University's Kogod School of Management, shows that more men are entering so-called female fields of work and are advancing more quickly. For example, men who enter the nursing profession are more likely to be promoted to a senior administrative role, than women with the same experience.

GLASS WALLS

According to Leonie Still, the glass wall is slightly different; it represents a barrier preventing a woman or a minority from moving to a position that is a lateral career move. A Wall Street Journal article of 1992 also reported on Catalyst's study on "glass walls" found in corporations. The cause of this phenomenon is due to historical reasons, stereotypes and cultural biases against minorities.

It also occurs due to unconscious biases that are embedded historical policies and processes (that were designed for men mainly) recruitment and leadership positions.

The antidote to this is to enable people raise their self-awareness and consistently fight these biases that are normally self-preserving beliefs that are selfish.

These biases are both conscious and unconscious and knowing how they appear and affect us will enable leaders redesign policies and processes that block competent minorities from growing.

GLASS LABYRINTH OR GLASS MAZE

Eagly and Carli, of Northwestern University and Wellesley College, argue in their 2007 Harvard Business Review article, 'Women and the Labyrinth of Leadership' that the glass ceiling metaphor has outlived its usefulness. This is because the concept leads managers to overlook interventions that would solve the root cause. They proposed that a labyrinth is a more fitting image to help organizations understand and address the obstacles to women's progress.

Rather than depicting just one absolute barrier at the top stage of a distinguished career, a labyrinth conveys the complexity and variety of challenges that can appear along the way for women and minorities. Thus, the glass labyrinth is a series of complexities, detours, dead ends and unusual paths. This research argues that women face a maze when trying to grow. This maze or labyrinth includes discrimination, women's domestic responsibilities, and sometimes women's own failure to believe in themselves.

BROKEN RUNG SYNDROME

The Women in the Workplace study, 2019 from McKinsey & Company and Leanin.org analyses women's experiences in corporate America building on data from the past four years. The research found that the broken rung is 'the biggest obstacle women face. This broken rung is on the path to senior leadership as its the first step up to manager.'

For every 100 men who are promoted to a first-time manager position, researchers found, only 72 women are. This shows that things are unequal at the door to managerial positions and that is where the problem lies.

The solution for this is not only for women to Lean In as Sheryl Sandberg said in her book but that they can also enlist male allies and organizations to meet them halfway. Companies can start by offering the same training, mentorship, and sponsorship offered to their male counterparts—at all levels.

Women also need more than mentors. They need equal sponsorship and promotion from their superiors—both men and women. Women can learn from how men subconsciously (and often consciously) are open to receive sponsorship and promotion through superiors, colleagues and out-of-office organizations.

An investment in women-only peer mentorship programs also grows the courage and confidence that they need to seek out, apply for, and get promoted.

THE PARETO PRINCIPLE WITH A GENDER LENS

Over my professional leadership journey spanning multiple sectors and locations, I have observed that when men apply for a promotion, they (on average) possess 20-60% of the skills needed while women will not apply unless they have 100% while they (on average) possess at least 80% of the required skills but perceive they only have 20% of the skills.

The solution is intensive coaching which helps women stay on track with accountability to keep advancing upwards and onwards with impact.

CLEAN GLASS DOOR SYNDROME

This is a phenomenon that occurs when people treat minorities as if they are invisible, just like people accidentally walk into a clean glass door, as they can't see the clean glass.

This syndrome is dehumanising and is seen when immigrants and minorities are trying to make ends meet through honest work which may be humbling but very vital.

This syndrome is also seen in our homes and families when parents treat their children with contempt and disregard their ideas.

It is also seen in our homes when we treat those who serve us in the domestic workspace without dignity.

The antidote is for each of us to remember that we all should treat others, as we would like to be treated.

We can also rethink how we look at work. Blue-collar work should not be despised. Those in influential positions should create cultures and opportunities for the minorities to contribute to in a more deliberate and positive way.

This will require more than a diversity agenda. It will require each leader to create a psychologically safe place for our teams and clients where people feel that they are seen, heard, and that their ideas and actions matter.

STICKY FLOOR SYNDROME

This metaphor according to Laabs, describes how some jobs prevent women (and some men) from moving out of certain positions. It refers to the largely invisible, unglamorous and low-level jobs in organisations which are essential to their smooth functioning, and which are predominantly occupied by women. Usually low paying, these jobs offer little prestige relative to others, and have only limited opportunities for promotion.

This means that once a woman is labelled as having a 'sticky floor' job, her ability to handle higher-level jobs is questioned. This results to old biases that hold back both women and men from ascending into new dynamic roles like STFM (Science, Technology, Engineering and Mathematics) for women.

QUEEN BEE SYNDROME

Queen Bee syndrome refers to women in authority or power who treat subordinate females worse than males purely because of their gender. TE Jayarante, C Tavris and GL Staines first documented this theory in 1973. Another academic study theorised that Queen Bee syndrome may be why women typically find it more stressful to work for female bosses than for male bosses. Also, the Queen Bee syndrome describes a woman who has personal and professional success but who refuses to share her knowledge and tips with other women to help them achieve their own success. Usually, queen bees fear that their group is not valued and instead distance themselves from their very own as they have internalized these biases and do not want to be associated with low status individuals.

THE OLD BOYS CLUB

This refers to the exclusively male network that accessed opportunities to lead and serve on boards without allowing other minorities such as women access to those opportunities.

However, there has been a shift towards more aware men being allies, mentors, leadership sponsors, and promoters for minorities. They do this for a higher purpose and for multi-generational impact as they have seen their children or grandchildren miss opportunities due to lack of access to the old boys club.

THE SHATTERED GLASS PHENOMENON

This is a more recent phenomenon referring to when a woman shatters the glass ceiling and navigates the glass labyrinth, other women see her as having achieved a significant milestone and celebrate the shattered glass while getting motivated to move forward and be their next best selves.

Unfortunately, many celebrate and forget that they still need to progress further to make the world a better place and workspaces more humane.

THE BOY CHILD CHALLENGE

This is an emerging challenge that is affecting young men. In some countries such as Kenya and other developing economies, there has been a significant focus on developing the girl child due to historical and cultural injustices. This focus is on levelling the playing ground. However, certain assumptions were also made in this progressive work, including:

- » That men will know how to relate with more self- aware and assertive ladies,
- » That men would be open to this new shifting paradigm of

women working outside the home,

» That men would not feel a threat to their identity of being the traditional breadwinner,

» That men knew all about leadership—yet more recently, many male leaders confess they do not have the same high level of skills and competencies that their fellow female counterparts have.

Having served on leadership panels where we interview talent, I have found that many young men lack the focus and confidence to articulate themselves. This may be because of the lack of clarity on their professional identity as well as their personal masculine identity. In some cases, they feel emasculated as the environment has radically changed and they do not know how to fit in. Unfortunately, due to the cultural background and upbringing where men were told not to show their emotions, they lack the courage to be vulnerable and to ask for help. When the inner turmoil persists, it sometimes explodes in the form of an amygdala hijack, which is when someone has not dealt with other historical emotional baggage and they explode at the smallest trigger. This sometimes causes violence and other negative coping mechanisms.

The solution is to equip men with life and leadership skills to strengthen their clarity of purpose and enable them to know that there is a connection between their masculine identity and their divine purpose.

Regardless of the opportunity blocker that you may experience, many times, your belief about yourself as well as your ability to position yourself as a professional solution provider makes all the difference. The important thing is to recognise what you are up against. Resolve it by not giving up and then, as far as it depends on you, create space for others to succeed. When you get to the leadership table, make it a personal commitment to make space by putting up a revolving or rotating door to enable others enter and serve to contribute to the inclusion dividend and to a more human culture and humane world.

Breakthrough Coaching

1. *Looking at all these syndromes discussed, examine which syndrome(s) are currently disabling your progress forward.*

2. *What can you do about it?*

3. *What do you commit to do after reading this chapter?*

Who's Got Your Back? Your Personal Board of Directors (BOD)

> Everything will line up perfectly when knowing and living the truth becomes more important than looking good.
>
> ~ **Alan Cohen**

Earlier on in my career, I struggled with perfectionism. I hired a coach and engaged a spiritual director to help me deal with the issue. Part of my discoveries was that many times, perfectionism is intertwined with a high sense of ego for a lot of high achievers. That was a painful realisation, but I was grateful that these members of my personal board of directors were keen to help me grow with sincere insights, and held my hand figuratively as I continued to overcome these tendencies.

Just like a company has a board of directors, we all need a personal board of a few trustworthy people who can give you a full view especially where you are unable to see solutions for growth and because we all have blind spots.

A personal board of directors or personal BOD, composed of two to four people, can provide you with the guidance and direction you need in your current season.

How do you create your personal BOD?

» Find and discern if you can trust them and that they are unafraid to give you feedback because they have your best interests at heart.

» Ensure that they have the same set of values and are committed to virtuously living those values.

» Assess them to confirm that they can see much further than you can because of their anchored, seasoned experience.

» Confirm that they are disinterested in your growth, meaning they will gain nothing from your growth and are detached from it.

» Check that they celebrate your success and keep challenging you to grow.

Be grateful for endorsers who speak positively about you in spaces where there are opportunities and possibilities for your growth and for you to provide a solution. Seek to develop more promoters in your network. Also seek to promote others.

Also, be wary of opposers who speak about you negatively and cast doubt about your abilities in meetings where you are not present. Understand why they see you in this negative light, make amends to your behaviour, as this may be important feedback and learn from the experience.

Finally, be alert to the fence-sitters, who have no reason to promote or oppose you. With sufficient motivation they can move into any of the other two camps. Understand that each of these three groups can influence your trajectory of growth but with wisdom, you can also influence how they perceive you. Your personal BOD are critical stakeholders in this process.

Breakthrough Coaching

1.   *Who will you appoint to your Personal BOD?*

2.   *Why do you need each person?*

3.   *What do you commit to do as a result of reading this chapter?*

Be a Bridge, Not A Ditch

You playing small doesn't serve the world. There's nothing enlightening about shrinking so others won't feel insecure around you. As you let your own light shine, you indirectly give others permission to do the same.

~ **Marianne Williamson**

Recently, we went to pay our last respects to a friend who had passed on. As I walked through the cemetery, I saw tombstone messages printed on the graves of those who have gone ahead of us, and I began to think about my own final moments, and what I would want written on my tombstone.

Soon after, I was hosting our BeAWiIlL (Breakthrough African Women in Intentional and Impactful Leadership) Global Network event and as I interviewed our leadership guest, I asked him what he would want written on his tombstone. Without skipping a beat, he said he would want them to write that he was a ladder, who in his lifetime had allowed people to climb up to grow.

What will be written on your tombstone? My hope for you is that you will choose to be a bridge and not a ditch.

Why a bridge? Because a bridge unifies, links, connects potential and reality. It enables people to connect with each other across different backgrounds. Good bridges are firm, anchored, and usually high over different locations. They provide those who use them with a different view and experience as they travel.

A ditch on the other hand, is the part of a road that causes people to fall in, accidents to happen, and generally, those who experience falling in a ditch tend to get hurt, get confused about their journey and sometimes lose their clarity of purpose for their future.

Being a bridge means being an intentional encourager. What if we decided to take the challenge and be intentional encouragers? The world has enough cynics, critics, and gloom dispensers already.

How can you be a bridge by being an intentional encourager?

1.   Ask for feedback from family members

I invite you to try a brief audit and ask your family members to describe you in one or two words. As you ask them for this feedback, take a glass of water and sip it as you listen to their feedback to ensure you are not defensive, because their truth and their perception matters because you've asked them for it. Note down and reflect on what they say. Encourage them to tell you the good, the bad, and the ugly aspects of your character because all these are facets of who we are, and when we know how we are affecting other people, something changes and shifts within us to make us improve and grow.

2. Seek the good in the people you live with

The easiest and most natural thing to do is to criticise the people we live with and work with. Instead, I would like you to try this: seek the good in them. I want you to hold back and catch them doing good. I was an auditor in the early days in my career, and part of the training was to look out for all the anomalies and things that are not working in an organisation. I know for many of us, catching people doing good is actually contrary to normal practice. Go contrary to your norm. Seek out the good in those around you. If you look carefully enough, you will find it.

3. Speak life-giving words

Choose to speak life-giving words. In one of our leadership programs, we talk about life-building words or life breaking words; others have called them words that diminish. I want you to now check your language as a third step and ask: How can I speak life into this person? Instead of being a gloom dispenser, one who just sheds darkness and discouragement on other people, let me choose to be a light dispenser.

During this COVID-19 pandemic, we have learnt to take care of our hygiene, and chances are, you have appreciated the use of dispensers, whether they are soap or sanitizer dispensers. I hope that whenever you wash your hands you will ask yourself, have I been an intentional encourager today? At the end of the day, you will look around you and begin to appreciate the far-reaching effects of your life-giving words and your choice to be an intentional encourager.

As we think about this experience, some of us may be struggling because we don't even speak words of encouragement to ourselves. How are you describing yourself during this crisis? Are you so disappointed with yourself that you haven't made some progress in certain things that you had hoped to do? Are you also asking yourself whether this is all doom? Check the quality of your self-talk. I encourage you to know that your journey is valid, irrespective of how tough and messy it is at the moment. This is the journey that we each must go through to forge and refine us, as we become our next best selves.

Dr Brene Brown, one of the foremost leaders and authorities in research around authenticity and vulnerability, and whose work I value, says if you are to talk to yourself like you'd speak to your best friend everything internally would shift positively. You're not likely to speak to your best friend and say something negative towards them. You're not likely to diminish them. You're not likely to help them ruminate over the negative things that have happened. What you're likely to do is encourage them and tell them to try again. Chances are that you're likely to actually speak to them and tell them to explore another angle. Check your inner thought world especially every morning when you wake up.

What are the words that you tell yourself? What are the words that you think about because the way you start your day makes a very big difference.

Also, the way you end your day has a very big effect on how you will encourage not just yourself, but others too.

As a family, we like to have a quick family get-together every evening and typically ask each other questions like, what was the highlight of your day? What's the lowlight of your day? How can I be of more support to you tomorrow? Recently, our daughter said to me: 'Mom when you played with me and we laughed, and you told me I could throw the ball very far you really lifted my spirits.' I probably would not have known that was a moment of encouragement for her as I was just getting on with a game and trying to encourage her to score. However, for her, that was the turning point in the game, when she saw that I believed in her and her ability to score.

How many opportunities are we missing out on to shed some sunshine on our family members and those close to us? Let us seize the moment.

I want you to take this a step further and think about your colleagues who you may or may not meet physically because you are working through phone calls, text messages, WhatsApp groups, and video conferencing facilities. When you look at your colleague through the video call do you see something positive that will encourage them during this time? When you call that colleague or that client, do you seek to lift their spirits and become an intentional encourager? Be the one who looks out for the quiet ones in the WhatsApp group, the ones who never speak up to check on them and encourage them.

Being a bridge not a ditch begins by encouraging yourself internally, because what we do internally always has a direct impact and effect on what we do externally.

BREAKTHROUGH COACHING

1. *Who have you been over the last 6 months? A bridge or a ditch?*

2. *What do you commit to do as a result of reading this chapter?*

We Only Rise By Lifting Others

> Simply shine your light on the road ahead, and you are helping others to see their way out of darkness.

~ **Katrina Mayer**

Every week, Michael Kinyugo commits to do a LinkedIn recommendation testimonial message for one of his professional contacts. His gesture inspired me, as I had not thought of lifting others so intentionally.

Another senior global leader Gianna Arthur is always being invited to serve on global boards and think tanks. Gianna carries with her a list of 10 exceptionally professional female leaders in her purse. When she is declining an invitation to a board of directors, she intentionally gives 3 names from her list and vouches for them. Over the years, she has positioned over 100 women leaders into board positions globally by using her strong recommendation.

Look at your hands, as you lift one hand to rise, the other should lift other people to rise so we can all rise sustainably.

How can you lift others? By mentoring them, teaching them, guiding them, positioning them for growth, having courageous conversations, and lifting them up in the best way you know how to.

How many fingers do you have? Attach a name to each finger, whether family members or professional contacts, reflect on what they need the most, and start enabling them to grow.

BREAKTHROUGH COACHING

1. *Who do you intend to lift up?*

2. *What do you commit to do as a result of reading this chapter?*

THE
FOURTH LEVEL

**The Power of Raising Yourself
for a Higher Purpose**

he fourth H is raising your entire self and being for a purpose that is greater than your individual existence. It means that you seek your purpose and calling in life so as to serve from a mission-centric perspective, and achieve transformational leadership through all the dimensions of life. This mission, to be impactful and authentic, can only be about others.

Pay Attention to Life's Whispers

When someone shows you who they are,
believe them.

~ **Maya Angelou**

I listened to Joy Jackson as she sobbed and narrated how she had been conned by a trickster. She recalled feeling something was not right in that land deal, but had ignored that feeling. She had noticed that the land seller was unable to look her in the eye. He would keep taking calls far away from her and was constantly agitated when she asked for more details. However, a good friend had introduced her to him so she opted to ignore her instinct and trust that her friend knew him better.

Now she had lost her life's savings to a conman because she did not pay attention to the whispers she experienced and did not trust her instincts.

Although we are to trust our instinct, we must remember, our instinct needs to be informed and educated because we all have a soft spot for something that may be bad for us.

How can we sharpen our ability to listen to life's whispers and form our conscience?

- » By reflecting on our experiences and others.
- » By aggressively listening to the said and unsaid.
- » By observing people and how they act and think
- » By journaling what we have learnt daily.
- » By seeking counsel from other wiser souls.
- » By reading wisely and widely to learn from different authors' experiences.
- » Most importantly, by examining why we do what we do, we get to the bottom of our hidden intentions.

Sakichi Toyoda, the Japanese industrialist, inventor, and founder of Toyota Industries, in the 1930s developed the five-why tool to unearth hidden intention. The 5 Whys technique became popular in the 1970s and is still used to date.

To examine if you are becoming a bridge or ditch, use the 5 Whys to check your inner intention and root cause. For instance, you may find you were over-critical towards someone.

» **Ask yourself the first why:** You may find its because you were irritated at them.

» **Then ask why 2:** you may find it is because they did something negative to you in the past.

» **Then ask why 3:** you may find it is because they hurt you and you had high expectations of them.

» **Then ask why 4:** you may find it is because you are bearing a grudge towards them and you haven't forgiven them.

» **Then ask why 5:** you may find it is because you are envious about their progress and when you compare yourself with them, you feel disappointed with yourself. Subsequently, you are behaving like a ditch.

Can you see how deeply discerning the 5 Whys technique can be? Get into the habit of checking your deeper motivations on 5 levels and accelerate your progress towards becoming a bridge not a ditch.

Breakthrough Coaching

1. How often do you pay attention to your instincts?

2. What has driven your behaviour?

3. What do you commit to do after reading this chapter?

Turn Your Deep Wounds into Deep Wisdom

> You learn things out of failure that take you further than success.
>
> ~ **John C Maxwell**

Too many people are stuck in their hurting past. They are grieving over a failure, a betrayal, a situation that did not go as they wanted it to go.

Jasmine Ting was such a vibrant person in the past but now she seemed to be a shadow of herself. What happened?

Jasmine got married and together with her husband Alan, they had difficulty having children. Having lost one child after another, she lost the zeal for life as she realised that the dream of being a mother was not forthcoming. She lost interest in her entire life, lost her job, and spiralled downward into a deep depression. After several years, and a lot of resistance, she finally gave in and saw a therapist. Over the last few weeks, she has started seeing light at the end of a dark tunnel.

Turning our pain into deep wisdom is not easy. It requires us to do the following five stages of turning wounds into wisdom, which I designed: Feeling. Dealing. Healing. Sealing. Revealing

THE PROCESS

Feeling means allowing yourself to face the pain, feel the deep hurt and recognise that you are struggling with something meaningful to you. It means being aggressively vulnerable with yourself, peeling the onion of emotions and getting to experience the range of emotions that are occurring within you. This step helps you move from denial to the angry stage in the Kubler -Ross Change Curve.

Dealing means finding out what is hurting you and what is the cause of your open wounds and hurting emotions. It means being brutally honest and applying the 5 whys to find out what is the root cause of your pain.

This journey can be complicated and sometimes we need professional help to face the truth. It is important to note that without facing the issue you cannot start the healing process.

Healing means allowing yourself to feel the pain again, to relive the experience, and objectively assess it to start seeing the lessons you were meant to gain from the painful experience. It is then that we start the process of curing our wounds. Many times, we are unable to heal because we blame ourselves and others for our misfortunes. If you believe in God, you will realise that everything happens according to His divine will for us and He allows even painful experiences for our greater good. He is also the all-powerful anchor and source of inner and outer healing.

Healing means letting go of the picture we had of how things would turn out and accepting the outcome as it is. But before that, you may need to go through the roller coaster of emotions as described by Kubler-Ross in their change curve. Knowing that you may yo-yo back and forth on the curve has given me comfort when struggling with healing and letting go. The aim in healing is to get to the point of acceptance of the pain.

Remember, many things in our past occurred because we did not know better. Now that we know better, once we heal, we will do better. Forgive yourself and others, but do not forget the lesson.

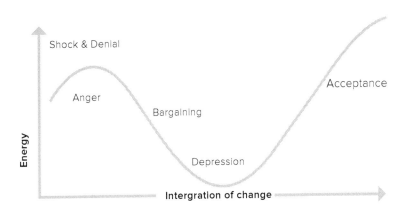

THE KUBLER - ROSS CHANGE CURVE

Sealing is the last phase of turning your wounds into wisdom. This is the process of metaphorically cleaning out the wound of any infection. Practically, this means allowing yourself to exhale and to try to put the issue behind you. It may mean that you choose to make some decisions such as raise boundaries or as Jasmine and her husband eventually did, they allowed themselves to dream a new dream and adopted 3 babies, welcoming them into their family and believing that a child is a gift, born from the womb or the heart.

Sealing means you choose to stop talking about the pain and crying about it and decide to focus on the lessons you gained. It may mean that you seek to understand that you are better off now than before that experience because you have gained clarity of purpose from the pain.

Time is a healer, only when we use it to get closer to healing. Once you deal, heal, and seal, you will be ready to help others who may be going through a similar issue and you will turn your wounds into wisdom for many through the final stage.

Revealing: This is the final stage that comes from renewal after inner healing and sealing. After going through the previous four stages, you will have your hope renewed once you have accepted the lessons you were to learn from the deeply painful experience.

Revealing means being wisely vulnerable to share the experience you went through with the perspective of the wisdom you gained and with the intention to encourage others with the painful lessons you went through to become your next best self. To get to this stage of revealing means being vulnerable to show yourself as you really are and to express how your wounds became wisdom that will not only help you. After all, I deeply believe that we go through tough painful seasons, not for ourselves but for others to learn from our pain and for us to encourage them in their dark seasons.

B<small>REAKTHROUGH</small> C<small>OACHING</small>

1. *Examine yourself over your current season, are you in any of the above five stages with respect to a painful experience?*

2. *What do you commit to do after reading this chapter?*

The Purpose Equation

> The purpose of life is not to be happy. It is to be useful, to be honorable, to be compassionate, to have it make some difference that you have lived and lived well.

~ **Ralph Waldo Emerson**

It took one look for me to see that the women in that company were being mistreated. They were not being given a fair chance to be who they were and to contribute justly to the company's agenda and strategy. The young talent, both male and female, were being exploited on the shop floor. That image could not leave my mind. I knew I had to do something about it. I had to work on a solution soon. That kind of work-life and company culture was not human or humane. Many years later, I realised that incident and my feelings towards it was the start of my journey of purpose.

It took me 15 years to figure out my purpose and the journey continues to unfold. I had to listen to the pain and frustration from within and then do something about it. I surrounded myself with mentors, as I have never been afraid to seek counsel and to reflect on other people's experiences.

Where your pain and passion intersect, that's where your purpose is: your big why. Each of us has a unique purpose to fulfil on earth with our lives.

Pain points are times in your life when you have experienced pain or have seen others experience pain and you realise that you have to find a solution because it relentlessly gnaws at your spirit. The pain of the experience does not disappear and instead keeps recurring until you pay attention to it.

Passion zone is the sum total of your gifts, talents, experiences, and skills that you do effortlessly and that take you to a space of flow. In a deep sense, our purpose is always going to be connected with our set of gifts and strengths.

Purpose zone: Our divine maker did not allow us to be born for nothing. Each of us has a divine assignment, a problem we are meant to solve and a courageous step we need to take to start to live our purpose.

When you combine your passion with your pain, at that point of intersection, you find your purpose.

Pain * Passion = Purpose

To apply this purpose equation, do the following:

Look back to any pattern of pain that keeps recurring and ask yourself, why is this issue so important to me?

Then ask yourself, what can I do with what I have to solve this issue?

Then start small but start today. Be consistent, and you will uncover your purpose: your divine assignment.

Our purpose is intricately connected to the purpose of others because our purpose is only about enabling others to move forward in the chosen space that calls at us. My calling has a name. My Name.

Your calling has a name. Your Name.

Answer the call and start to live a meaningful life.

Sadly, if we choose not to answer this call, we disconnect ourselves from our calling and disconnect others who are only connected to their calling and purpose through us.

When we do not start doing something about our purpose, we risk many others not getting to uncover their purpose as they are linked to us finding and doing something intentionally about our purpose.

BREAKTHROUGH COACHING

1.   *Examine yourself. Is there a deep pain that is begging for your attention?*

2.   *Which skills and talents are you using for a higher mission to solve that problem?*

3.   *Is there anything you would do without being paid for it because of how meaningful it is to you?*

4.   *What do you commit to do after reading this chapter?*

Who Are You Accountable to?

A leader without accountability will rarely
have a purposeful impact.

~ **Dr Patricia Murugami**

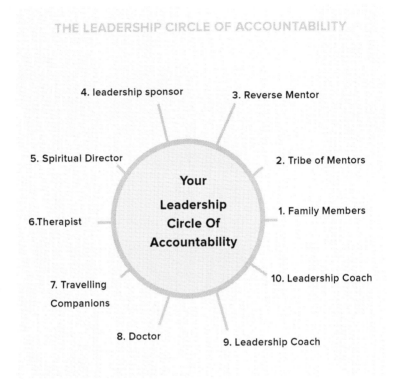

© Dr Patricia Murugami

When I was completing my doctorate, I found that I had to raise my accountability if I intended to finish well while ensuring my number one priority, my family, did not bear the brunt of my studies and research. I realised that I could not do it alone.

I also realised there were many well meaning points of advise that were not aligned to my values and purpose. I recall one lady telling me to relocate and leave my family for a year to finish the rigorous doctorate. I knew that this was not aligned to my values and commitment to my husband and children so I chose not to take that advise.

Another one told me to postpone having children until I was Dr Murugami. I smiled and told her that I was aware that having children was a time bound critical process while completing the doctorate could be postponed. More importantly, what I did not tell her is that we struggled with having children and had decided with my husband from the moment we got married (now almost 20 years ago), that we were open to having all the children God wanted us to have, and the doctorate was not going to stand in the way of the gift of children and our calling as a married couple and parents.

The profound lesson of knowing my glass balls (these are time-bound important goals critical to my season and values) and knowing my rubber balls (these are flexible goals that could be postponed) was clarified by leaning into a leadership accountability circle before, during and after I successfully defended and completed my doctorate.

With the gift of foresight, I selected a global postgraduate school that would not penalise me for taking a leave of absence in the event that we were blessed with another child. And as the miraculous blessing of growing a family would have it, I excitedly took a two-year break in between the doctoral research stage to have our second-born daughter. I still recall her sitting next to me drawing her childlike artistic drawings as I collated my extensive research, analysed it and completed my thick thesis while our older daughter asked me questions about my hypothesis and findings. My mother and father were so attuned to my doctorate that I knew I was on the right track. Talk about doing a doctorate as a family project! I continue to be deeply grateful.

I cannot underestimate the value of having a strong leadership accountability circle to rely on and whose members are keen to see you grow and thrive.

There is another member of the accountability circle who deserves a mention: our house assistant. Were it not for her and the critical role she played in helping me run our home well while I studied, worked, and as I prioritised my non-delegable role of being wife and mother, I would not have managed.

I still remember the day I successfully defended my thesis and they were praying quietly for my results. When I came out and shared the news of my success, she quietly said, 'Congratulations! You have worked so hard. When you are ready, may we discuss a change in my contract? I was waiting for you to become Dr Patricia Murugami and then we would discuss my intention to resign and go to get married.'

I was moved beyond tears that she had subordinated her goals so that she could support me to meet mine. That's what a genuine leadership accountability circle member does.

Who do you need to grow exponentially of the 10 members in the leadership accountability circle?

Let's examine who the 10 members are:

1. Family members

These are the people who are part of your family of origin or the family you have procreated. They include parents, siblings, spouse, children, parents-in-love, siblings-in-love (others call them in-law, I prefer to call them in-love as love came before the law of marriage) and any other members of your family. For some people, they have a spiritual family also and they should also be included in this group.

Family members are usually not afraid to tell you where you are going off and how you can improve. Because of their close proximity to us, they see our struggles and imperfections daily, and as such, make excellent accountability partners.

My husband has been such a powerful accountability partner since I met him two decades ago and now during this book writing journey. This book has been a family project from the moment I shared with him and our children of my desire to publish. Because of that vulnerability, we did it! The book is in your hands. That's the power of family accountability.

When I look back to all the key risky decisions I have taken in my career to follow my purpose, there is no way I could have taken those decisions without his wise input and insights.

2. Who is in the tribe of mentors?

Many people mistakenly think that they should have only one mentor and this curtails their growth. I learnt the term tribe of mentors from Tim Ferris in his book **Tribe of Mentors.** The tribe of mentors depicts a range of mentors including those who have your best interest and others who may not know they are your mentors.

A good mentor is a tour guide who has been there and is willing to walk you through the leadership journey with a spirit of generosity. A good mentor is not a travel agent who has never walked the journey you are experiencing. From my experience, a tribe of mentors is made of several people:

» **Seasoned mentor**: one who has experienced life, usually older than you.

» **Author mentor**: one who has experienced what you want to learn and has written about it.

» **Peer mentor**: one who is at your level professionally and you symbiotically and mutually learning from each other.

» **Accountability mentor**: one who knows your goals intimately and holds you accountable without judgement.

How many ways can you be mentored?

» Author mentorship: through books you read.

» Spot mentorship: through observation of how your mentors act.

» Virtual mentorship: through digital platforms like YouTube.

3. Reverse mentor: one who is younger than you and is mentoring you about new skills like ICT, social media, the internet of things and other new skill sets in the future of work. Normally, these younger people want to be mentored by you but it's time to reverse the order of mentorship.

In many ways, these reverse mentors are our children, nephews, nieces, and live in our homes or work with us as interns. Be humble and ask them to teach you something even as you mentor them.

4. Leadership sponsor

A leadership sponsor is one who sees your excellent work and takes a reputational risk on you by speaking about you in spaces you have no access to so as to lift you to grow. They position you for your next step of growth.

5. Spiritual director

This is someone who you can trust to guide your soul and spirit based on your faith and spirituality.

6. Therapist

This is a professional who is trained to help you mend and heal from trauma. Ensure you choose one who has the values you hold dear to you.

7. Travelling companions

These are few friends who are close to you, like your foundation and pillar people, who travel the journey of life with you. To keep these friends you need to invest time, money, energy and prayer.

8. Doctor

This is a trained and certified medical doctor who you entrust with knowing your medical history and physical well-being.

9. Executive Coach

This is a certified professional whose sole agenda is to move your goals forward in a psychologically safe space using coaching techniques.

10. Professional Networks

These are professional groups who meet for a mutually beneficial cause to improve their level of knowledge and become better professionals.

What do you need to be held accountable and rise?

- » An open and sincere mind
- » A coachable and learning spirit
- » Wise vulnerability to share your struggles
- » Authenticity to explain your season and the values you are trying to live
- » A kind heart to share your lessons with others
- » An attitude of gratitude to give feedback on your progress
- » The culture of writing down your resolutions and progress

Vulnerability and humility is critical as well as having mindful competence. These will enable you to grow deeply.

Finally, you are only as good as the people you surround yourself with, choose wisely.

BREAKTHROUGH COACHING

1. *Who do you need the most during this season?*

2. *What do you commit to do as a result of reading this chapter?*

How Much Rent Are You Paying for Being on Earth?

> Your greatest test is when you are able to bless someone else while you are going through your own storm.
>
> ~ **Unknown**

A story is told of an old man, Babu, teaching his grandson about life. 'A fight is going on inside me,' he said to the boy. 'It is a terrible fight and it is between two wolves. One is evil—he is anger, envy, sorrow, regret, greed, arrogance, self-pity, guilt, resentment, inferiority, lies, false pride, superiority, and ego.'

He continued, 'The other is good—he is joy, peace, love, hope, serenity, humility, kindness, benevolence, empathy, generosity, truth, compassion, and faith. The same fight is going on inside you—and inside every other person, too.'

The grandson thought about it for a minute and then asked his grandfather, 'Which wolf will win?'

Babu simply replied, 'The one you feed.'

It is said that we build legacy by what we do daily, whether knowingly or not, consciously or subconsciously. The rent we pay for being on this earth ought to be intentionally doing good deeds that are of service to society.

As we end our journey together and you see your next best self emerge, I would like to encourage you to plant a tree selflessly, even if you know you may never sit under its shade. Plant it for other generations.

Planting a tree does not mean the actual tree (though that also counts) it means actions that are positive with a multi-generational impact.

It means that we stop chasing success, which tends to be like chasing the wind, and instead focus on being significant, which means serving others outside of our comfort zone. It means building others and being a building block not a stumbling block.

To do this and raise your rent, I encourage you to consider the following two suggestions:

i. Let go of anything that no longer serves your soul

I have found that to pursue my purpose, many distractions and temptations have come my way. I have given in to some and conquered myself in others.

More recently, I have seen that before a meaningful encounter to follow my purpose and serve others, I have usually besieged with negative situations that on the face of them seem positive.

I have realised that as you follow your purpose relentlessly for a higher purpose, you must be ready to go through a breakdown before you attain your breakthrough. You have to be ready to go through turbulence to die to yourself and as a result birth a new version of yourself.

You may ask: how do you let go of that which no longer serves your soul? Setting yourself free and letting go is one of the hardest things you may have to do.

Practically, it means the following:

» Raising boundaries where previously you had not developed any between you and the person(s) or situation you need to let go of.

» In some cases, it means untying the bond to loosen it and not cut off.

» In other cases, it means cutting off completely from the situation.

» It also means letting go of your expectations of the situation or person.

Until you are ready to let go of that which no longer gives you peace, your progress towards your purpose will be a moving unattainable target.

Remember that temporary success can distract us from purposeful significance if we choose to see success as an end in itself.

Significance is all about being other-centred while success can easily be about self-centredness.

ii. Ways of raising the rent you are paying for being on earth

» Take stock of your gifts with a spirit of gratitude.

» Choose to share what you have and know generously.

» Align what you do in private to what you do in public—have internal personal congruence, which results in unity of life.

» Detach yourself from needing the affirmation of others.

» Let go of that which no longer serves your soul's peace.

» Practice daily forgiveness.

» Have a beginner's mind-set and coachable spirit.

» Become your next best self continuously and spread this message of lifting the 4 Hs to as many as you know.

» Once you start doing this, get ready to re-introduce yourself as your next best self having raised your heart, head, and hand all for a higher purpose.

BREAKTHROUGH COACHING

1. What are you doing today that future generations will benefit from?

2. What do you commit to do after reading this chapter?

THE POWER OF RAISING YOURSELF ON THE FOUR LEVELS FOR A HIGHER PURPOSE

When I first moved out of my parent's home, I was so proud to pay rent for my first bedsitter in one of the popular estates in Nairobi that I could not wait for my first night in my very own house. It did not matter that it was a small house, it was mine.

As I lay down to sleep smiling at my accomplishments of buying a bed and a few other household items, I thanked God and felt deeply asleep.

At about 3am, I suddenly heard the rustling of my unpacked shopping paper bags and fearfully woke up to put on the light and check what was about to attack me.

As I put on the light from the corner of my eye, I saw the largest cockroach I had ever seen! It looked as if it could bite off my toe! With hindsight, it must have been genetically modified.

I knew that as they normally react, cockroaches like darkness and when the light is on, they scatter for safety. So I spent the rest of the night with the light on waiting for morning so that I would buy a pesticide and alert my landlord to fumigate the house.

What did I learn? That we all have dark secrets, struggles, breakdowns, fears and pains in us. We all have 'cockroaches' in a sense that are plaguing our peace and purposeful progress.

However, we must face these and put on the light to dispel the cockroaches and then metaphorically fumigate. This is by trusting someone, reading an insightful message and putting new ideas into action.

Looking back, my life has been such a journey. Writing this book has been another journey. I realise that each journey leads us in the direction of becoming our next best selves. However, it all depends on the choices you and I make as we have been granted the free will and intellect to do that. To grow in a holistic way using the $G=H^4$ formula requires each of us to be intentional in raising our heart, head, and hand for a higher purpose.

To rise, we need to take stock of where we are and to learn from the painful breakdowns we have had, both public and private. Those moments when we have doubted deeply, yet hope has arisen after the darkest night as sure as the sun rises every morning.

I am reminded of how my journey to finding my purpose was full of debates, crossroads, and risky transitions. I wondered about my study and career choices and whether I would succeed. I prayed about my vocation and wondered how to be faithful to my calling.

When I was in the dating phase, I wondered if he was the one until I finally found him, my husband (of almost two decades to date), George Murugami. I fondly remember our rainy wedding day and the sunshine we had in our hearts at the prospects of turning our ordinary family life into something extraordinary.

I recall the dark season of losing our babies on earth but on the other hand, knowing with faith that they had gained heaven and would pray for us daily.

I recall the deep joy and ebullience on the birth of our children after a season of hope and detachment as we waited for the gift of children. What an amazing miracle life is.

I remember the risk of taking several career choices without being sure of the outcome except that the choices would move me closer to finding and living my purpose.

I remember the naysayers' voices as they berated me, shamed me, and caused me to doubt myself when I allowed myself to pay attention to them.

I remember the countless moments of deep peace and meaning when something I did made a difference to someone. When through a class, a Breakthrough leadership circle, a social media post, a coaching session or through a simple conversation, I had the unmerited privilege of lifting another person's spirit for a higher purpose.

And because of this, every breakdown led to a breakthrough not only for me but for many others too.

I have made peace with the fact that in our lives we may never know how our work positively impacts others. But if we have the positive intention of consistently rising from our comfort zones and lifting others, then it will have a multi-generational impact for a much higher purpose.

As you can see, my life has been full of crossroads and reflections, wondering if I am on track, but that is life.

I am deeply grateful for all the good, bad and painful experiences as each were meant to help me grow and become my next best self.

I hope that as you read this book, you have seen that raising your heart requires you to be fully vulnerable to yourself and then wisely vulnerable to those you trust.

I hope you have realised that to raise your head you require intellectual humility, deep honesty, and a coachable spirit.

I hope that you have seen that raising your hand for yourself and more importantly, to lift others requires you to be self-assured and be magnanimous.

And to do this means you are raising yourself for a higher purpose, which is a journey of beginning again daily with hope and faith.

May this 4-way manifesto for a meaningful life give you the affirmation to feel and know that you are worth it and that your journey so far is valid and is leading you to where you are meant to go.

May you repeat often the following affirmation, which forms my daily note to self:

I am worthy.

I have potential.

I have possibilities.

I am a child of God.

I am valid. I am invaluable.

My ideas and words matter.

I am intentionally becoming my next best self for a higher purpose.

My final prayer for you as you embark on your very personal unique journey to becoming your next best self is:

That each day, you may be granted the courage to raise your heart,

That each day, you may have the clarity of purpose and competence to raise your head;

That each day, you may have the confidence to raise your hand and magnanimity to raise the hands of others;

That each day you may have the discernment, wisdom, and detachment to raise yourself for a higher purpose.

Here's to you becoming your next best self.

Rise! And let the journey begin.

References

Ali, H. (2001). More than a hero: Muhammad Ali's life lessons presented through his daughter's eyes.

Brown, B. (2012). Daring greatly: How the courage to be vulnerable transforms the way we live, love, parent and lead. Bren Brown. Hay House.

Covey, S. R. (2015). The 7 habits of highly effective people: Powerful lessons in personal change. Mango Media.

Covey, S. R. (2015). Covey's circles of influence —The DP Learning Zone — Development Partnership Learning Zone (2015, June 24) . https://dplearningzone. the-dp.co.uk/2015/06/24/coveys-circles-of-influence/

Escrivá, J. (2017). The Way. Scepter Publishers.

For women, glass ceilings, and glass walls, too. (2016, November 16). The New York Times - Breaking News, US News, World News and Videos. https://www. nytimes.com/2016/11/16/opinion/for-women-glass-ceilings-and-glass-walls-too. html

Forbes. https://www.forbes.com/sites/jennagoudreau/2012/05/21/a-new-obstacle-for-professional-women-the-glass-escalator/?sh=211bbd00159d

Glass Ceiling or Sticky floor. (2017, March 2). Women In Power. https:// womeninpower.org.au/glass-ceiling-or-sticky-floor-barriers-to-careers-of-women/

Guise, S. (2015). How to be an Imperfectionist: The new way to self-acceptance, fearless living, and freedom from perfectionism. Selective Entertainment LLC.

Harvard Health Publishing (n.d.) 'Giving thanks can make you happier'.

Harvard Health Publishing (2019, September 24). In praise of gratitude. Harvard Health. https://www.health.harvard.edu/mind-and-mood/in-praise-of-gratitude

Helgesen, S., & Goldsmith, M. (2018). How Women Rise: Break the 12 Habits Holding You Back. Random House.

Laterbox. (2015, April 28). 8 types of procrastinators. Medium. https://medium. com/@laterboxapp/8-types-of-procrastinators-448a8d7cbc07

Learning Agility - What It Means For Employees, Leaders And Businesses. (2018,

*July 30). Chief Learning Officer - CLO Media. https://www.chieflearningofficer.
com/2018/05/16/learning-agility-role-leadership/*

Meyer, J. (2012). Approval Addiction. Hachette UK.

*Meyer, J. (2014). The Approval Fix: How To Break Free From People Pleasing.
Hachette UK.*

*Mind the (Skills) Gap. (2012, September 21). Harvard Business Review. https://hbr.
org/2012/09/mind-the-skills-gap*

*Murphy, A. (2009). Leadership & Organization Development Journal, 30(2), 167-
182. https://doi.org/10.1108/01437730910935800*

*The Navarre Bible: The Wisdom Book : the Books of Job, Proverbs, Ecclesiastes
and the Wisdom of Solomon in Sirach in the revised standard version and new
Vulgate. (2004). Four Courts Press Ltd.*

*(n.d.). Online Resources I. https://edge.sagepub.com/system/files/15_
GlassCeiling.pdf*

*Phillips, K. A., Singh Ospina, N., & Montori, V. (2019). Physicians interrupting
patients. Journal of General Internal Medicine, 34(10), 1963-1963. https://doi.
org/10.1007/s11606-019-05141-0*

*Press, P., & I, F. (2014). Praying with my Fingers: An Easy Way to Talk with God.
Paraclete Press.*

Rath, T. (2007). StrengthsFinder 2.0. Simon & Schuster.

*Ryan, M. K., & Haslam, S. A. (2005). The Glass cliff: Evidence that Women
are Over-represented in Precarious Leadership Positions. British Journal of
Management, 16(2), 81-90. https://doi.org/10.1111/j.1467-8551.2005.00433.x*

Sandberg, S. (2013). Lean In: Women, Work, and the Will to Lead. Knopf.

*Self-care has never been more important. (n.d.). https://www.apa.org. https://
www.apa.org/monitor/2020/07/self-care*

*Sheryl Sandberg on the Myth of the Catty Woman. (2016, June 23). The New
York Times - Breaking News, US News, World News and Videos. https://www.
nytimes.com/2016/06/23/opinion/sunday/sheryl-sandberg-on-the-myth-of-the-
catty-woman.html*

*Tracy, B. (2008). Eat that Frog!: 21 Great Ways to Stop Procrastinating and Get
More Done in Less Time. ReadHowYouWant.com.*

149

VUCA world - Leadership Skills & strategies. (2020, August 16). VUCA-WORLD. https://www.vuca-world.org/

(n.d.). https://eprints.lse.ac.uk/65859/1/Glass%20ceilings.pdf

What is Queen Bee Syndrome? (2013, July 26). HRZone. https://www.hrzone.com/hr-glossary/what-is-queen-bee-syndrome

(n.d.). Wo.Men.Hub. https://gwmh.org/wp-content/uploads/2019/03/2017-Patricia-Murugami-DBA-Dissertation-Final-31-October-2017.pdf

Women in the Workplace 2019: The State of Women in Corporate America. Lean In. https://leanin.org/women-in-the-workplace-2019

DR PATRICIA MURUGAMI is a global leadership catalyst, an award-winning speaker, certified transformational coach, leadership educator, and the founder and CEO of Breakthrough Leadership Transformation. She is also an ITC-SheTrades Global consultant specialising in crisis management, leadership resilience, and new normal strategies.

Dr Murugami holds a Doctorate in Business Administration-Transformational Leadership and Governance from the International School of Management in Paris, France. She also holds a MBA from University of Nairobi and is a Certified Public Accountant (CPA-K).

Dr Murugami has served on multiple boards and is a sought-after board advisor and executive team leadership coach. She is passionate about inclusive leadership and has enabled many women and other minorities in East Africa serve as executive and board directors. Her work has been honoured with awards including Top 40 under 40, 2010; Jacob's Well Most Impactful 12 Women in the Region, 2015; and the National Diversity & Inclusion Business Executive Champion Award, 2019. She hosts the you-tube channel Breakthrough with Patricia Murugami and the weekly leadership podcast: Your Next Best Self.

Patricia is joyfully married to Murugami, and together, they are intentionally bringing up their children and mentoring many for a multi-generational impact.

Contact the Author at:

 @Dr Patricia Murugami   @patmurugami

 lead@bltgroup.co.ke   www.bltgroup.co.ke

Printed in Great Britain
by Amazon